国家国际科技合作重大项目（KY201801004）
国家国际科学和技术合作北马其顿专项（2017511） 联合资助
甘肃省国际科技合作项目（7YF1WA157）

INTRODUCTION TO TRANSFER OF TECHNOLOGY IN UNIVERSITY

大学技术转移概述

中英双语版

［中国］张国锦
［北马其顿］Ivan Bimbilovsky
［北马其顿］Elisabeth Spiroska ◉ 著
［中国］李 欣

蘭州大學出版社
LANZHOU UNIVERSITY PRESS

图书在版编目（CIP）数据

大学技术转移概述 = Introduction to Transfer of Technology in University : 汉英对照 / 张国锦等著. -- 兰州 : 兰州大学出版社, 2021.5
ISBN 978-7-311-05990-3

Ⅰ. ①大… Ⅱ. ①张… Ⅲ. ①高等学校—技术转让—研究—汉、英 Ⅳ. ①G644

中国版本图书馆CIP数据核字(2021)第092066号

责任编辑 武素珍
封面设计 汪如祥

书　　名	大学技术转移概述 Introduction to Transfer of Technology in University
作　　者	张国锦 Ivan Bimbilovsky Elisabeth Spiroska 李 欣 著
出版发行	兰州大学出版社 (地址:兰州市天水南路222号 730000)
电　　话	0931-8912613(总编办公室) 0931-8617156(营销中心) 0931-8914298(读者服务部)
网　　址	http://press.lzu.edu.cn
电子信箱	press@lzu.edu.cn
印　　刷	西安日报社印务中心
开　　本	710 mm×1020 mm 1/16
印　　张	8.75
字　　数	165千
版　　次	2021年5月第1版
印　　次	2021年5月第1次印刷
书　　号	ISBN 978-7-311-05990-3
定　　价	26.00元

BRIEF INTRODUCTION TO EDITORS
作者简介

Mrs Zhang Guojin(Oct.1967-), An associate researcher of public relations and majored in International Relations Studies. Chinese nationality from Qingyang Gansu Province. She currently work at the school of international education, Lanzhou Jiaotong University Gansu Province P.R. China. She is the Director of the International Science and Technology Cooperation Base for Infrastructure Construction of the Gansu Provincial Science and Technology Department. She was appointed as the Director of Laboratory, China Gansu-North Macedonia Science, Technology and Culture Exchange Center. She was a visiting scholar of University of Alberta in Canada and University of Worcester in UK. She presided over the 4 projects of the Ministry of science and technology of China in the area of the international science and technology cooperation. She was awarded the prize of "the four kinds of talents" of International Communication of Gansu Province; the second prize of science and technology progress of Gansu Province; the Talas Shevchenko by the Ministry of education of Ukraine. She has published more than 20 papers.

张国锦（1967.10—），公共关系学副研究员，中国国籍，甘肃庆阳人。现就职于兰州交通大学国际教育学院。甘肃省"一带一路"基础设施建设国际科技合作基地主任，中国甘肃—北马其顿科技文化交流中心实验室主任。加拿大阿尔伯塔大学、英国伍斯特大学访问学者。甘肃省"四个一批"国际传播人才。主持科技部国际合作项目四项。获甘肃省科技进步二等奖、乌克兰教育部"塔拉斯·舍甫琴科"奖。发表论文20余篇。

Dr. Professor Ivan Bimbilovsky(July 1974-), Professor. North Macedonia Nationality from Skopje. He is currently the president of the University of Information Science and Technology in North Macedonia. He is a member of the Council of the national academic research network of Skopje in North Macedonia. He was a visiting professor of the University of the Walailak University, Nakhon Si Thammarat, Thailand, a Senior Fellow of the Higher Education Academy, York, United Kingdom researcher of the University of higher education, York, UK., and a senior visiting scholar of Lanzhou Jiaotong University. He has published more than 50 papers.

伊万·比姆比洛夫斯基（1974.07—），博士，教授。北马其顿国籍。现任北马其顿信息科学与技术大学校长。北马其顿斯科普里国家学术研究网络理事会成员。泰国纳洪西塔马拉特瓦莱拉克大学客座教授，英国约克郡高等教育学院高级研究员，英国高等教育大学高级研究员，兰州交通大学高级访问学者。发表论文50余篇。

DR. Elisabeth Spiroska(May 1979–), associate professor. She was born in 1979 in Ohrid, North Macedonia, who was graduated from the University of Skopje in North Macedonia and had received her doctor's degree in law from the "St. Cyril and Methodist Church". She is currently an associate professor, secretary general and EKTS coordinator of the Saint Nicholas University of international education in North Macedonia. Dr. Elizabeth spiroska has a lawyer's qualification certificate, works as a lawyer and mediator, and serves as legal adviser to law firms, non-governmental organizations and other organizations. She also works as the vice chairman of the ethics committee of the association of mediators of the Republic of North Macedonia. She has published more than 20 papers and two university textbooks in international journals and conferences in North Macedonian and other countries.

伊丽莎白·斯皮罗斯卡（1979.05—），博士，副教授。北马其顿国籍。现任北马其顿圣尼古拉斯国际教育大学副教授、秘书长和EKTS协调员。拥有律师资格证书，从事律师和调解员工作，并担任律师事务所、非政府组织和其他组织的法律顾问，北马其顿共和国调解人协会道德委员会副主席。在北马其顿等国发表论文20余篇，出版大学教材2部。

Li Xin (Aug. 1981-), lecturer, master of Computer Science. Chinese nationality from Qingyang Gansu Province. He currently work at the school of international education, Lanzhou Jiaotong University Gansu Province P. R. China. He is mainly engaged in the filed of Computer Science and Technology. He was a visiting scholar of the University of Massachusetts at Boston, USA and the University of Marjebel, Slovakia. He has published five academic papers.

李欣（1981.08—），计算机科学与技术硕士，讲师。中国国籍，甘肃庆阳人。现就职于兰州交通大学国际教育学院。主要从事计算机科学与技术领域的研究。美国波士顿马萨诸塞大学、斯洛伐克马杰贝尔大学访问学者。发表学术论文5篇。

PREFACE

It is generally recognized that technology transfer plays a key role in the economic and industrial development of any country and that technology transfer is also seen as an essential strategic variable that must be incorporated into national development planning. This book is an overview based on the results of the technology transfer of the China–North Macedonia project. The book focuses on the basic operations and concepts of some of the issues involved in the technology transfer in universities to help researchers and professionals in enterprises and technology transfer institutions discuss and assess the potential of their research and development technology, help them market innovations, obtain development funds and promote university - enterprise cooperation. This book also introduces some fundamental issues that researchers and businesses should understand and some ways to commercialize research or technology.

The authors of this book are all participants engaged in cooperation, communication, teaching and research between China and North Macedonia in recent years. The book consists of an introduction, six chapters and a conclusion in English. The first and second chapters are written by Zhang Guojin; the following chapters are written by Ivan Bimbilovski and Elizabeta Spiroska, and the conclusion is written by Li Xin. The Chinese version of this book is written and translated by Zhang Guojin. The book is compiled and revised by Zhang Guojin and Li Xin.

This book is a compilation, in addition to our own research results, but also cited a large number of domestic and foreign research results. In the process of writing, based on our scientific research and exchange and cooperation work, we strive to express clearly the relevant contents of the transformation of Chinese and foreign technology transfer. Still, in the face of complex Chinese and foreign differences and a wide range of literature, the omission is inevitable, hope expert and reader give advice, make it prefect day by day.

Editor

1st May 2021

Lanzhou China

前　言

众所周知，技术转移在任何国家的经济和工业发展中都发挥着关键作用，技术转移也被视为一个国家重要的发展指标，应当被纳入国家发展规划。本书是基于中国—北马其顿项目技术转移成果的概述，重点介绍大学技术转移所涉及的基本概念和操作，以帮助企业和技术转移办公室的研究人员与专业人员讨论和评估其研究和开发技术的潜力，帮助他们进行市场创新，获得发展资金，促进大学与企业的合作。

本书的作者主持参与了中国与北马其顿项目的合作、交流、教学和研究，实践经验丰富。全书由七个章节组成，英文文本导言、第一章和第二章由张国锦撰写，第三章、第四章、第五章和第六章由伊凡·比姆比洛夫斯基（Ivan Bimbilovsky）和伊丽莎白·斯皮罗斯卡（Elisabeth Spiroska）撰写，结论由李欣撰写。中文文本由张国锦翻译与撰写。全书由张国锦、李欣统编和修订。

本书是一本汇编，除作者的研究成果外，还引用了大量国内外的研究成果。在本书撰写过程中，作者立足于自身的科研和交流合作工作，力求清晰表达中外技术转移的相关内容，但面对复杂的中外差异与广泛的文献，笔下疏漏在所难免，敬希专家同行和读者不吝赐教，使之日趋完善。

编者

2021年5月1日

中国兰州

CONTENTS

目　录

ABBREVIATIONS
英文缩写释义

ARIPO	African Regional Intellectual Property Organization	非洲区域知识产权组织
AUTM	Association of University Technology Managers	大学技术管理人员协会
CDA	Confidential Disclosure Agreement	保密披露协议
EPO	European Patent Office	欧洲专利局
EU	European Union	欧洲联盟
GDP	Gross Domestic Product	国内生产总值
ID	Invention Disclosure	发明披露
IP	Intellectual property	知识产权
IPRs	Intellectual property rights	知识产权
NDA	Non-Disclosure Agreement	非披露协议
OECD	Organization for Economic Co-operation and Development	经济合作与发展组织
PCT	Patent Cooperation Treaty	专利合作条约
SMEs	Small and medium enterprises	中小企业
TT	Technology Transfer	技术转移
TTO	Technology Transfer Office	技术转移办公室
UNICO	University Companies Association	大学企业协会

1 BASIC UNDERSTANDING OF TECHNOLOGY TRANSFER

1.1 What is "technology transfer"?

There are many definitions of technology transfer, partly because the term has many different connotations,[①] partly because the technology transfer is not the same process and perception for everybody (universities, researchers, corporations, developed countries, developing countries).[②] For example, most universities and research organizations consider technology transfer as the transformation of scientific research into products with wider commercial use and benefits to society. On the other hand, companies' technology transfer by companies is a business opportunity to gain higher profits and become more competitive.

Technology transfer can be defined as a process of transferring scientific discoveries, innovations, technologies, skills, knowledge, methods of manufacturing, samples of manufacturing (prototype, demonstrator, sample products), facilities from one institution or country to another for further development or commercialization.[③] In general, technology transfer refers to all transformations of research to products.

---

① See: Choi, H.J., 2009. Technology Transfer Issues and a New Technology Transfer Model. *Journal of Technology Studies*, 35(1):49-57.

② Ibid.

③ World Property Intellectual Organization. *Technology Transfer in Countries in Transition: Policy and Recommendations Division for Certain Countries in Europe and Asia*:3.

第一章　技术转移的基本概念

1.1　技术转移的定义

技术转移有许多定义[①]，一是因为这一术语有许多不同的含义，二是因为不同主体（如大学、研究人员、公司、发达国家、发展中国家等）对技术转移过程的看法并不相同[②]。例如，大多数大学和研究组织认为，技术转移是将科学研究转化为具有广泛的商业用途和社会效益的产品，而公司的技术转移则被视为去获得高利润，更具竞争力的商业机会。

技术转移可以定义为将科学发现、创新、技术、技能、知识、制造方法、制造样品（原型、演示品、样品产品）和设施等从一个机构或国家转移到另一个机构或国家，以进一步开发或商业化的过程[③]。一般来说，技术转移是从研究到产品的所有转换形式。

① See: Choi, H.J., 2009. Technology Transfer Issues and a New Technology Transfer Model. *Journal of Technology Studies*, 35(1):49-57.

② Ibid.

③ World Property Intellectual Organization. *Technology Transfer in Countries in Transition: Policy and Recommendations Division for Certain Countries in Europe and Asia*:3.

Technology transfer is a process and typically includes a set of components: identifying innovations with commercialization potential; protecting innovation through patents, copyrights, or other ways for the protection of intellectual property; creating and developing the commercialization pathways; adverting of the innovation, and licensing to existing companies or building new start-ups or spinoff companies based on the innovation.[①]

The process involves a variety of players such as funding states or private agencies, universities, research and transfer organizations, venture capitalists and private companies and individual scientists, entrepreneurs and business angels.[②] The success of the technology transfer process depends on the interaction among these actors and their capabilities to overcome the barriers.

There is no doubt that the technology transfer process depends and, at the same time, is based on the policies and culture of each country and each institution. In this framework, the economic, political, and socio-cultural factors are of particular importance for the technology transfer process and its success.

The long-term goal of the technology transfer is to increase economic growth by transferring innovations from science to commerce.

1.2 The types of technology transfer

Technology transfer comes in different types.[③] It involves a variety of formal and informal means: informal interactions between individuals, workshops, personnel exchanges, collaborative research, publishing, consulting, standardization, hiring of graduates, joint projects involving groups of experts from different organizations, patenting, copyright, licensing, forming of new companies, contract research and

① See: European Union European Regional Development Fund, 2016. *Report on national understanding of transfer processes and reference model of transnational transfer*.

② Karlsson, M., 2004. *Commercialization of Research Results in the United States—an Overview of Federal and Academic Technology Transfer.* ITPS, Swedish Institute for Growth Policy Studies: 15.

③ See: Kundu, N., Bhar.C. and Pandurangan, V., 2015. Development of Framework for an Integrated Model for Technology Transfer, *Indian Journal of Science and Technology*, 8(35).

技术转移的过程通常包括以下环节：确定具有商业化潜力的创新；通过专利、版权或其他保护知识产权的方式保护创新；创造和发展商业化途径；对创新进行宣传；向现有公司发放许可证或根据创新建立新的创业或分公司①。

这一过程包含各种参与者，如资助国家或私人机构、大学、研究和转移组织、风险资本家和私营企业以及个人科学家、企业家和天使投资人②。技术转移成功与否取决于这些行为体之间的互动及其在这一进程中克服障碍的能力。

毫无疑问，技术转移进程取决于并同时以每个国家和每个机构的政策和文化为基础。在这一框架中，经济、政治和社会文化因素对技术转移进程至关重要。

技术转移的长期目标是通过将创新从科学转移到商业中，来促进经济增长。

1.2 技术转移的类型

技术转移有不同的类型③。它包含各种正式和非正式手段，如个人之间的非正式互动、讲习班、人员交流、合作研究、出版、咨询、标准化、毕业生的雇用，不同机构专家组参与的联合项目，专利、版权、许可、组

① See: European Union European Regional Development Fund, 2016. *Report on national understanding of transfer processes and reference model of transnational transfer*.

② Karlsson, M., 2004. *Commercialization of Research Results in the United States—an Overview of Federal and Academic Technology Transfer*. ITPS, Swedish Institute for Growth Policy Studies:15.

③ See: Kundu, N., Bhar.C. and Pandurangan, V., 2015. Development of Framework for an Integrated Model for Technology Transfer, *Indian Journal of Science and Technology*, 8(35).

more.①

The primary distinction is made between vertical technology transfer and horizontal technology transfer. Vertical technology transfer occurs when information is transmitted from basic research to applied research, from applied research to development, and from development to production.② Horizontal transfer of technology occurs when technology used in one place, organization, or context is transferred and used in another place, organization, or context.③

Technology transfer takes place along various lines: among universities, from universities to industry, from governments to industry, across borders.

1.3 University technology transfer

1.3.1 Definitions of university technology transfer

University technology transfer is a process of knowledge exchange between university and industry. This is a process where two sides, researchers and universities on one side and individuals or companies on the other, exchange learning, ideas and experiences.④ Researchers from different universities and industries/businesses shape different kinds of collaborations to develop the knowledge or transform the knowledge into technology. This collaboration results in various benefits for both sides, but the most important benefit is knowledge exchange itself, and it should be viewed and discussed as quality from the start to the end of the technology transfer process. The process of knowledge exchange/technology transfer also helps develop the early-stage intellectual property into tools for direct use by the research community or into bases for new platforms, products, or services to be made into products

①Organization for Economic Co-operation and Development (OECD), 2013. *Commercializing Public: New Trends and Strategies*: 18–21.

② See: Mansfield, E., 1982. *Technology transfer, productivity, and economic policy*. Norton.

③ Ibid.

④ Digital Agenda for New Tourism Approach in Europe Rural and Mountain Areas, available at http://www.danteproject.eu/?q=Exchange.

建新公司、合同研究等[①]。

技术转移也可分为纵向技术转移和横向技术转移。纵向技术转移发生在信息从基础研究传递到应用研究，从应用研究传递到产品开发，或从开发传递到生产的过程中[②]。横向技术转移指在一个地方、组织或系统中使用的技术被转移到另一个地方、组织或系统中，并被使用[③]。

技术转移还可按照途径分类，如大学之间、大学到产业之间、政府到产业之间或国与国之间的技术转移。

1.3 大学技术转移

1.3.1 大学技术转移概要

大学技术转移是大学与产业之间知识交流的过程。这是一个双向的过程：一面是研究人员和大学，另一面是个人或公司，双方交流知识、想法和经验[④]。来自不同大学和行业或企业的研究者形成了不同类型的合作，来开发知识或将知识转化为技术。这种合作给双方带来了诸多好处，但最大的好处是知识交流本身，从技术转移过程的开始到结束，都应将其视为重点并加以讨论。知识交流或技术转移过程还有助于将早期阶段的知识产权开发成为供研究团队或机构直接使用的工具，或成为供大众使用的新平

① Organisation for Economic Co-operation and Development (OECD), 2013. *Commercialising Public: New Trends and Strategies*:18-21.

②See: Mansfield, E., 1982. *Technology transfer, productivity, and economic policy*. Norton.

③ Ibid.

④Digital Agenda for New Tourism Approach in Europe Rural and Mountain Areas, available at http://www.danteproject.eu/?q=Exchange.

for public use.[①] Technology transfer protects the intellectual property rights of the university, too. The university, as a part of the technology transfer process, can decide for the retention of the technology intellectual property rights, therefore to conclude agreements concerning the licensing of technology. Successful technology transfer produces and develops numerous benefits for inventors, universities, businesses, as well as society and region. The revenue from the technology transfer for the universities supports education, further research and also influences the university's reputation and public trust in the university. On the other hand, the industry deals with money losses and opportunity costs which can be reduced as a result of the licensed technology. And, as one of the most important issues, university's investments in technology help stimulate local economic development.

University technology transfer was defined in the recent *McMillan Report* on good practice in technology transfer as: "the commercialization of university-owned research outputs through the licensing of intellectual property rights (patents, copyrights, know-how, databases and design rights) to existing companies and setting up new spin-out companies"[②] In other words, university technology transfer is a development process where scientific findings are converted into commercially valuable products.

The successful transfer of new technologies from the research laboratory to the commercial sector has many benefits, such as creating wealth, new jobs and new solutions to society's problems.[③] In this regard, it should be noted once again that university-technology transfer produces benefits for both, the universities that have to

①Lenagh, A., 2012. The importance of technology transfer, available at https://www.unemed.com/blog/the-importance-of-technology-transfer, accessed 22 September 2020.

② HEFCE., 2016. *University Knowledge Exchange (KE) Framework: good practice in technology transfer: Report to the UK higher education sector and HEFCE by the McMillan group*: 11.

③ See: Fisher, L.M., 1998. The innovation incubator: Technology transfer at Stanford University. *Strategy and Business*: 76–86; Sherer, T., 2014. Technology transfer contributes multiple benefits to universities; AUTM 2017 Licensing Activity Survey available at https://autm.net/surveys-and-tools/surveys/licensing-survey/2017-licensing-activity-survey, accessed 22 September 2020.

台、产品基础，或是成为为制造产品而服务的基础[①]。技术转移也保护了大学的知识产权。大学作为参与技术转移中的一分子，可以决定是否保留技术知识产权，从而缔结关于技术许可的协议。成功的技术转移为发明者、大学、企业以及社会和地区的发展带来了诸多好处。一方面，大学技术转移的收入，可以用于支持教育，进一步支持科学研究，也会提高大学的声誉和公信力。另一方面，企业可以借助大学技术转移降低研发成本，提高经济效益。最重要的是，大学对技术的投资有助于刺激当地经济发展。

《麦克米伦报告》中将大学技术转移定义为：通过向现有公司发放知识产权（专利、版权、技术、数据库和设计权）以及设立新的分公司的方式[②]，将大学所拥有的研究成果进行商业化。即，大学技术转移是一个将科学发现转化为具有商业价值产品的过程。

成功地将新技术从研究实验室向商业部门的转移意义重大，例如能够创造财富和新的就业机会，为解决社会问题提供新方案等[③]。同时，由于自身发展的多种需求，大学必须在教育和研究之间取得平衡，而企业

①Lenagh, A., 2012. The importance of technology transfer, available at https://www.unemed.com/blog/the-importance-of-technology-transfer, accessed 22 September 2020.

② HEFCE., 2016. *University Knowledge Exchange (KE) Framework: good practice in technology transfer: Report to the UK higher education sector and HEFCE by the McMillan group*: 11.

③ See: Fisher, L.M., 1998. The innovation incubator: Technology transfer at Stanford University. *Strategy and Business*: 76–86; Sherer, T., 2014. Technology transfer contributes multiple benefits to universities; AUTM 2017 Licensing Activity Survey available at https://autm.net/surveys-and-tools/surveys/licensing-survey/2017-licensing-activity-survey, accessed 22 September 2020.

balance education and research because of different types of demands, and businesses that continuously seek ways to make money.

1.3.2 Institutions and mechanisms of university technology transfer

The university-technology transfer process is assisted by institutions known as technology transfer offices (TTO). Their names may differ: Technology Licensing Office, Technology Transfer Office, Licensing Office, Office of Intellectual Property, Office of Innovation and Commercialization and so on.[①]

During this process, the usually used mechanisms are patents and other modalities for the protection of IPRs, licenses, and spinoffs or start-ups.

① Costas, I., Euro, A., Echarri, J.M., Piqué, R. and Condom, P., 2012. From research to market: key issues of technology transfer from public research centers to businesses. *Imprimeix SL*: 61.

则不断寻求提高产值的方法。所以，大学技术转移对出让方和受让方都有益处。

1.3.2 大学技术转移的机构和机制

负责承担大学技术转移职能的机构通常可称为技术转移办公室，也可称为技术许可办公室、许可办公室、知识产权办公室或创新和商业化办公室等[①]。

大学技术转移过程中涉及的常用机制有：专利管理和其他保护知识产权的方式、许可证管理和附带利益管理以及初创企业等。

①Costas, I., Euro, A., Echarri, J.M., Piqué, R. and Condom, P., 2012. From research to market: key issues of technology transfer from public research centres to businesses. *Imprimeix SL*: 61.

2 TECHNOLOGY TRANSFER OFFICE AS A MODALITY FOR UNIVERSITY TECHNOLOGY TRANSFER

2.1 What is TTO?

TTOs are organizational structures that come in various types, but always with the same main aim: to assist research organizations (including universities, faculties, research institutes, etc.) in the process of transformation of innovation into benefits for society. TTOs are products of the necessity for the effective management between universities and business/industry in favor of making new products along with insurance that all the participants in the transfer process will obtain sufficient rights and monetary benefits.

TTOs are devoted to overcoming divergences in the process of practical exploitation of science. The aim is to play a supportive function closely related to research activities to improve technology transfer efficiency.[①] They are actually a passage for finding the most appropriate and the most effective way for technology transfer.

2.2 TTO activities

TTO's elementary scope of activities includes protecting intellectual property rights and commercializing inventions whose commercialization potential was previ-

① See: University of Luxembourg, Technology transfer, available at https://wwwen.uni.lu/snt/technology_transfer_office, accessed 20 September 2020.

第二章 技术转移办公室
——大学技术转移模式

2.1 技术转移办公室的定义

不同国家、不同实体的技术转移办公室的组织结构虽然不同，但主要职能趋同，即：在将科研创新转化为社会效益的过程中为研究机构（包括大学、学院、研究所等）提供援助。技术转移办公室是大学和企业或产业之间有效管理的必要产物，有助于生产新产品，同时保证所有转移过程的参与者都将获得足够的参与权和经济效益。

技术转移办公室有助于化解科技研发过程中的分歧，为研究活动提供密切相关的、有针对性的支撑服务，从而提高技术转移的效率[①]。也就是说，技术转移办公室是技术转移得以实现的最适当、最有效的方法。

2.2 技术转移办公室的工作

技术转移办公室的工作范围包括保护知识产权，并将具有商业化潜力

①See：University of Luxembourg，Technology transfer，available at https://wwwen.uni.lu/snt/technology_transfer_office，accessed 20 September 2020.

ously evaluated. But the essential precondition for any other TTO activities is researchers' information about the existence of their innovation for TTO. However, there are at least two TTO activities expected by the founders of a TTO:

• To lead researchers and universities to determine the commercial value of innovation during the process and help them with the documentation through the technology transfer process.

The first formal communication between researcher and TTO is the disclosure of invention made in a written form. This document should be uncomplicated and easy to use for the researcher; it should not contain detailed information, just needed information. Regarding the details, there is always time for detailed information through the upcoming communication with the researcher. TTOs and universities should be aware of the fact that the complicated model of invention disclosure document could be an obstacle for the participation of the researchers in the technology transfer process.

• To evaluate commercial potentials of innovations.

Basically, TTOs are founded to manage the gap between the researchers/universities and businesses/industry in respect of finding commercial and/or industrial applications for innovation. TTOs are not connected to the scientific value of the innovation but to its commercial value. The evaluation of the commercial value of innovation is, without doubt, one of the most important parts of the TTO's field of operation, and it is not an easy task. In literature and practice, there are many procedures, techniques and viewpoints for the evaluation of innovation. The evaluation process is especially important because it sets the basics for the successful technology transfer process and directions for later decisions connected with the process itself as well as with the rights of the participants in the process. TTO may decide that the innovation is not suitable for commercialization, but in this case, the TTO is obliged to process all the activities in a way to ensure that researchers or others interested in the commercialization of the innovation can do so.

TTO activities as specified operations are related to different stages within the technology transfer process, but they can be divided into three basic groups as fol-

评估过的研究成果商业化。技术转移办公室运作的先决条件是：研究人员向技术转移办公室提供其创新发明成果的全部资料，技术转移办公室则应承担如下主要工作：

• 在技术转移过程中，引导研究人员和大学确定创新的价值，帮助相关人员准备必要的材料。

研究人员和技术转移办公室之间的第一次正式交流应采取书面形式介绍发明成果。这份书面文件应简洁明了，便于研究人员使用，且只包含必要信息，而非详细信息。复杂的发明成果介绍可能会给研究人员参与技术转移造成障碍。所以，第一次正式交流不应过多涉及发明成果和技术转移细节问题的沟通。

• 评估创新的商业潜力。

从根本上来说，建立技术转移办公室是为了拉近研究人员或大学与企业或产业在寻找商业和产业创新应用方面的距离。技术转移办公室与创新的科学价值无关，而与其商业化价值有关。对创新商业化价值的评价无疑是技术转移办公室经营领域中的首要任务之一。我们从研究和实践中发现，对创新的评价有许多不同的程序、方法和观点。其中，过程评价尤为重要，因为它为成功的技术转移过程奠定了基础，为以后与该技术转移进程本身以及与该进程参与者的权利有关的决定指明了方向。技术转移办公室可以判定发明成果不适合商业化，但在这种情况下，技术转移办公室也有义务完成所有工作，使得研究人员或其他对创新商业化感兴趣的人能够知晓商业潜力缺失的具体原因。

按照技术转移过程的不同阶段，技术转移办公室的工作可分为三项基

lows: disclosing, secure IP rights and commercialization.

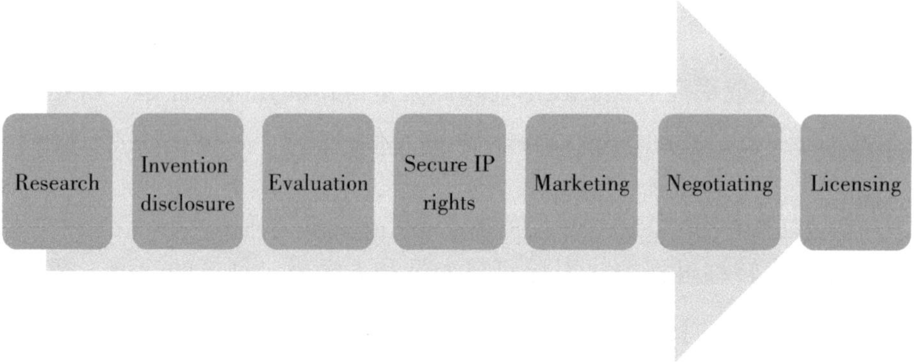

Figure 1 Technology Transfer Office Activities

2.3 Disclosing and assessment

2.3.1 Invention disclosure

TTO activities start by disclosing the invention. What does it mean? It means that the inventor/researcher identifies his/her invention or discovery (any new helpful process, machine, composition of matter, or any new or useful improvement of the same, discoveries, research tools, processes, know-how, or software that may solve a significant problem and/or have significant value, hereinafter: invention). A very important notice for researchers is to be aware that at this stage of the technology transfer process, the invention does not have to be already prepared for the market.

The first step for starting the relationship between the researcher and TTO is Invention Disclosure (ID). The ID is a written description of the invention which is brought to TTO. As previously said, ID should be user-friendly for researchers, but there are some necessary information which should be included: how the invention is created; how it is reproduced; the importance of the invention; why it improves on current works; its advantages over prior work; its scope of use; the list of all the contributors (the principal investigator, responsible manager, research assistants, students, staff, visiting scientists), all academic or other research institutions and/or

本操作：发明披露、知识产权保护和商业化。

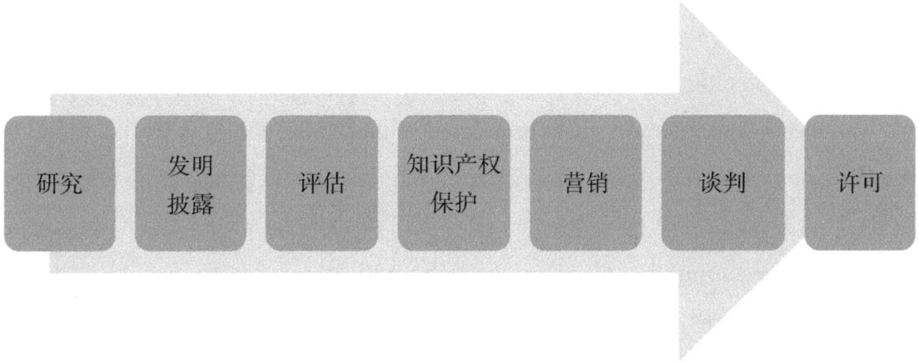

图1 技术转移办公室的工作

2.3 发明披露和评估

2.3.1 发明披露

技术转移办公室的工作是从发明披露开始的，即：发明者或研究人员确认并公布发明或发现。发明或发现（以下简称：发明）包括实用的新过程、新材料、新硬件，或新的改进、研究工具、方法、技术和软件等。值得研究人员注意的是，在技术转移过程的这一阶段，发明没有必要对市场做好准备。

建立技术转移办公室与研究者联系的第一步是发明披露（ID）。发明披露是提供给技术转移办公室的发明的书面描述。如前所述，发明披露便于研究人员和技术转移办公室使用，但也应该包含一些必要信息，如发明的历程、目的、重要性，发明的优势与创新性，发明的使用范围，发明的参与者（主要研究者、责任经理、研究助理、学生、员工、访问

companies; third-party arrangements if there are any; any publication connected to the inventions. It is obvious that these facts are necessary for TTO to realize whether there are and what are the potential paths for the commercialization of the innovation. Researchers should be aware that the ID is a confidential document. It is also a necessary document because it is the way in which the researcher confirms his/her approval for TTO to offer its help throughout the technology transfer process.

The next very important question related to the ID is: When is the best time for ID to be completed? The prevailing notion is that anytime is a good time to complete the ID. However, according to the majority of TTOs, the best time for completing an ID is before presenting the discovery through publications, poster sessions, conferences, press releases, publications on the Internet, abstract, non-confidential research proposal, or other communication. Researchers want to show the world their innovations. Nevertheless, they should be aware that when the invention is already familiar to the public, it often blocks the patenting and commercializing opportunities. Therefore, the researchers should disclose their inventions to TTO and will be helped with all needed information about the "publication freedom" of their invention. On the other hand, it does not absolutely mean secrecy: researchers usually could disclose some parts of their inventions (such as main results and description of the problem.). Considering the previous statement, researchers should contact the TTO in the early research phase to discuss the unknown topics related to the commercialization of the invention in the future, and these discussions will also guide researchers to obtain the desired results.

Every TTO has developed its own form of ID, but the features described above are common for most TTOs. Usually, ID forms and instructions for ID are available in Word format on the TTO's website.

2.3.2 Evaluation (assessment) of the invention

After receiving an ID, TTO starts activities that could promote the commercialization of the invention. The first step in these activities is the evaluation of the invention: The team of the TTO transfer agency first reviews disclosure of the invention, evaluates the marketability and patentability of it, and determines its commercializa-

学者）、研究机构、公司，第三方协议（如果有的话）以及与发明有关的出版物等。显然，这些书面描述能使技术转移办公室认识到创新商业化的潜在途径。研究人员也应该知道，发明披露是一份机密文件，也是一份必要的文件，因为这是研究人员授权技术转移办公室在整个技术转移过程中提供服务的主要依据。

与发明披露相关的另一个非常重要的问题是，发明披露完成的最佳时机。一种较为普遍的说法是，任何时候都是完成发明披露的好时机。然而，根据大多数技术转移办公室的实际操作经验，完成发明披露的最佳时间是在通过出版物、海报论文展示、会议、新闻稿、互联网、摘要等非机密研究成果披露之前。研究人员在向世界展示其创新的同时也应该意识到，当发明为公众所知晓时，专利化和商业化的机会往往会受到阻碍。因此，研究人员应该向技术转移办公室披露他们的发明，提供其发明“出版自由”的所有必要信息。由于发明披露的过程并不是绝对保密的，研究人员通常可以披露其发明的某些部分，例如主要成果、问题描述等。综上所述，研究人员应该在早期研究阶段就与技术转移办公室联系，以便与技术转移办公室及时讨论未来工作中遇到的、与发明的商业化有关的未知问题，这些讨论也将有助于研究人员获得满意的技术转移结果。

不同的技术转移办公室都有各自的发明披露形式，但上述特性仍是大多数技术转移办公室的共同特征。有关发明披露的形式和操作的Word格式文件可在技术转移办公室的网站上获得。

2.3.2 发明的评估（考核）

在收到发明披露材料后，技术转移办公室正式开始工作，来促进发明的商业化，而在技术转移办公室的工作中，第一步则是评估发明。技术转移办公室团队首先要审查发明披露内容，评估发明的可营销性和可专利

tion process. At the same time, it evaluates its relationship with relevant intellectual property rights, the scale and growth of the potential market, and also conducts necessary patent search, estimates the cost and time required for further development, the existing rights related to intellectual property rights as well as the potential competition from other products or technologies. TTO should always keep in communication with inventors.① In short, the evaluation process should answer the question of whether or not a specific invention is suitable for commercialization. The answer to this question is based on the ID and other information gained from the researcher throughout discussions, interviews and other communication.

There are numerous frameworks and models for evaluating the commercial value of the innovation,② but some of the most important criteria are divided into four categories, as shown in Figure 2.③

① See: NC State University Office of Research Commercialization at https://research.ncsu.edu/otcnv/for-inventors/inventors-guide-to-technology-transfer/, accessed 20 September 2020.

② See: Mohannak, K. and Samtani, L.A., 2014. A criteria-based approach for evaluating innovation commercialization. DRUID Society Conference 2014, CBS, Copenhagen, June 16–18, available at https://conference. druid. dk/acc_papers/i1xk9l9pli4jnefryvacrvpjdy22. pdf, accessed 20 September 2020; Estep, J. and Daim, T., 2016, September. A framework for technology transfer potential assessment. *In* 2016 *Portland International Conference on Management of Engineering and Technology* (*PICMET*):2846–2852.

③ See: Mohannak, K. and Samtani, L.A., 2014. A criteria-based approach for evaluating innovation commercialization. DRUID Society Conference 2014, CBS, Copenhagen, June 16–18, available at https://conference. druid. dk/acc_papers/i1xk9l9pli4jnefryvacrvpjdy22. pdf, accessed 20 September 2020.

性，确定其商业化过程。同时，评估发明与相关知识产权的关系，评估潜在市场的规模和增长，开展必要的专利搜索，评估进一步开发所需的成本和时间、与知识产权相关的既存权利，以及评估来自其他产品或技术的潜在竞争。技术转移办公室还应始终与发明者保持沟通[①]。总之，评估过程应回答某一发明是否适合商业化的问题。这个问题的答案基于发明披露以及研究人员在整个讨论、访谈和其他交流过程中获得的其他信息。

评估创新商业化价值[②]有不同的框架和模型，但其中最重要的标准可分为四类，如图2所示[③]。

① See：NC State University Office of Research Commercialization at https://research.ncsu.edu/otcnv/for-inventors/inventors-gue-to-technology-transfer/, accessed 20 Sepetember 2020.

② See：Mohannak, K. and Samtani, L.A., 2014. A criteria basedcriteria-based approach for evaluating innovation commercialisationcommercialization. DRU ID Society Conference 2014, CBS, Copenhagen, June 16–18, available at https://conference. dru. dk/acc_papers/i1xk9l9pli4jnefryvacrvpjdy22.pdf, accessed 20 September 2020; Estep, J. and Daim, T., 2016, September. A framework for technology transfer potential assessment. *In* 2016 *Portland International Conference on Management of Engineering and Technology* (*PICMET*):2846–2852.

③See：Mohannak, K. and Samtani, L.A., 2014. A criteria based approach for evaluating innovation commercialisation. DRU Society Conference 2014, CBS, Copenhagen, June 16–18, available at https://conference.dru.dk/acc_papers/i1xk9l9pli4jnefryvacrvpjdy22.pdf, accessed 20 September 2020.

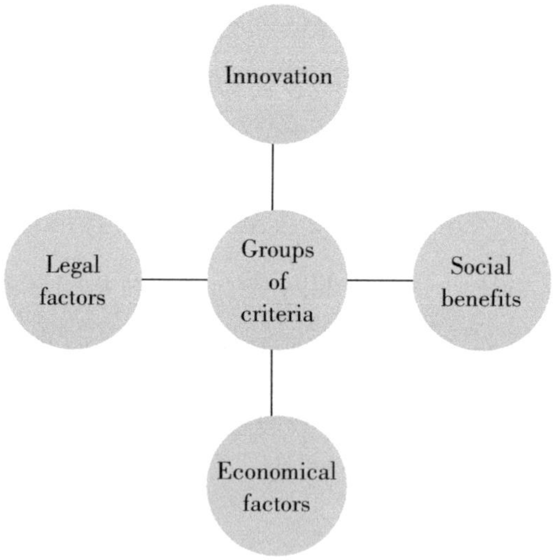

Figure 2 Groups of criteria for evaluating the commercialization value of the innovation.

Each of these four groups consists of elements which have an influence on evaluating the commercial value of the innovation. These elements are shown in Table 1.

Table 1 Elements for evaluating the commercialization value of the innovation

Innovation	replicability, complexity, scope for alternate applications, ready or not theory, proof of application in practice, incriminatory potential with other innovations; prototype availability innovation feasibility, potential for further development
Legal factors	knowledge spillover, creation of employment, enhancement of social infrastructure/networks, environmental impact, cost advantages to customers, brand recognition, potential for new useful applications
Economical factors	contribution to economic growth/development; potential for attracting required resources, for example venture capital; potential return on investment; market entry; distinguishable competitive advantages; market impact; level of competition; time to market
Social benefits	protection of IP rights, strengths and scope of patent including geographical extent, patent exclusivity, new areas of application, need for complimentary technologies; freedom to operate

Source: Mohannak, K. and Samtani, L.A., 2014.

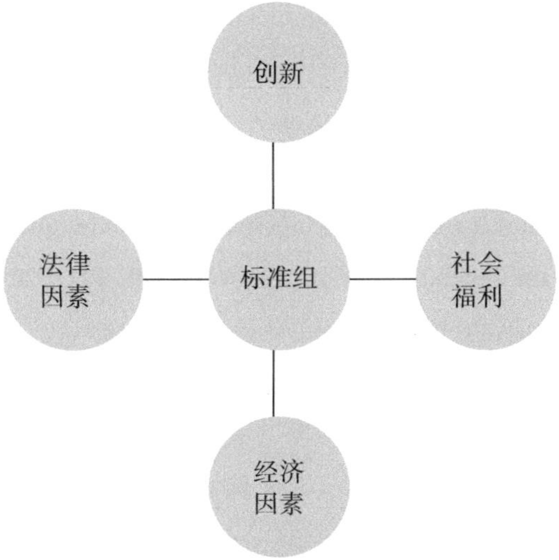

图2 评价创新商业化价值的标准组

上述每组因素都由影响创新商业价值评估的要素组成，评价要素如表1所示。

表1 创新商业化价值的评价要素

创新	可复制性；复杂性；替代申请的范围；理论的完备程度；实践中应用的证明；与其他创新结合的潜力；原型可用性；创新的可行性；进一步发展的潜力
社会福利	知识溢出；创造就业；提升社会基础设施/网络；环境影响；对客户的成本优势；品牌认知度；新的有价值的应用的潜力
经济效益	对经济增长或发展的贡献；吸引所需资源的潜力如风险投资资本；潜在投资回报；市场准入；明显的竞争优势；市场影响；竞争水平；上市时间
法律因素	知识产权保护；专利的优势和范围，包括地理范围；专利豁免；新的应用领域；运作自由；对互补技术的需求

资料来源：Mohannak，K.和Samtani，L.A.，2014年。

It is preferable that TTO have established a time frame for carrying out the assessment process. The evaluation process can bring to one of the following three decisions: not proceeding: if the invention does not have commercial potential, the inventor continues the research; further development: if the invention shows commercialization potential, but it is still not ready for the commercialization or IPRs protection, in which case the inventor continues to work with TTO; and proceeding: TTO pursues intellectual property protection and pursues commercialization.[①] This process of selectivity ensures that TTO accepts the investment risks associated with IP protection and prosecution.[②]

We noted that the evaluation process is not easy at all for the TTO. In this regard, besides others, the evaluation process should also set the basic directions of the TTO's strategy for commercialization: already existing company or a new start-up.

2.4 Protection of the invention

The next activity after the evaluation is the protection of the invention. The protection of the invention includes trade secrets, trademarks, copyrights and patents. When it comes to protecting innovations and making profits from them, TTOs most usually apply for patents. Patent protection is maybe the adequate solution. One of the reasons for this solution is that patent protection is often a requirement of a potential commercialization partner (licensee) because it can protect the commercial partner's sizable investment required to bring the technology to market.[③] On the other hand, the patent serves as an incentive, giving the inventor privileges concerning

① Utah State University. Office of Research, available at https://research.usu.edu/techtransfer/process/.

② See: EMORY University Office of Technology Transfer available at http://www.ott.emory.edu/inventors/process.html, accessed 21 September 2020.

③ See: University of California, Berkeley, 2019. *An Inventor's Guide Technology Transfer, Berkeley IPIRA Intellectual Property & Industry Research Alliances*: 14.

技术转移办公室需要确定开展评估进程的时间框架。评估发明进程后可做出以下三项决定：(1) 不进行商业化：如果发明没有商业潜力，发明者则继续进行研究；(2) 进一步发展：如果发明显示出一定的商业化潜力，但仍未准备好商业化或知识产权保护，这种情况下，发明者继续与技术转移办公室合作；(3) 进行商业化：技术转移办公室应寻求知识产权保护及发明的商业化[①]。这种具有选择性的过程可确保技术转移办公室承担与知识产权保护和起诉相关的投资风险[②]。

对技术转移办公室来说，评估过程并不容易。在这方面，除去其他因素，评估过程还应确定技术转移办公室商业化战略的基本方向，即：通过现有公司或建立新的初创公司。

2.4 发明的保护

发明评估之后的下一项活动是发明的保护。发明保护包括商业机密、商标、著作权和专利的保护。当涉及保护创新并从中获利时，技术转移办公室通常会申请专利，专利保护是最合适的解决方案。因为专利保护往往是潜在商业化合作伙伴（被许可方）的一项常规要求，它可以保护商业合作伙伴为将推向市场所需的技术进行大量投资[③]。另一方面，专利作为激

①Utah State University. Office of Research, available at https://research.usu.edu/techtransfer/process/.

② See: EMORY University Office of Technology Transfer available at http://www.ott.emory.edu/inventors/process.html, accessed 21 September 2020.

③ See: University of California, Berkeley, 2019. *An Inventor's Guide Technology Transfer, Berkeley IPIRA Intellectual Property & Industry Research Alliances*: 14.

the exploitation of technology invented and therefore motivates innovation.①

The patent provides the right to exclude others from practicing the invention. However, patent protection is not possible for all intellectual property rights because numerous conditions must be met to obtain a patent. So TTOs seek another form of protection. The good news is that TTO is not limited to seeking creative and low-cost mechanisms for protecting work and/or invention in any stage of the research process. The webpage of some TTOs also gives visitors an introduction to trade secrets, trademarks and copyrights. We consider this solution as a useful tool in many ways. Researchers will have a better understanding of ways to protect their work and innovation, and encourage them to disclose their results to TTO. For TTO, it is one of the effective ways to promote their work, that is, to develop, protect, transfer and commercialize research results for the public interest. That is a way we suggest that the website of TTO should outline some of the considerations that are important in trade secrets, trademarks and copyrights issues.

As previously mentioned, a common legal protection method used by TTO is patent. Patent protection begins with the filing of a patent application. In this regard, a very important question arises: "Who is responsible for patenting?" Patent documents and procedures are complex, so when preparing a patent application and files, the application within the relevant office, legal assistance is not only advisable but necessary. This problem with necessary legal assistance is resolved by TTOs in one of the following two ways: with in-house attorneys or counsels; or with outside patent specialists/counsels/law firms. The second solution is recommended because it secures the best possible patent specialists in a particular area, and it is cost-effective. The researchers should be aware that the specialist can write the patent application, but they work together with the patent specialist during its drafting.

After the patent application is prepared, it is submitted within the relevant office and follows by the procedures which differ significantly from country to country.

---

① Costas, I., Euro, A., Echarri, J.M., Piqué, R. and Condom, P., 2012. From research to market: Key issues of technology transfer from public research centers to businesses. *Imprimeix SL*: 18.

励，能够给予发明者开发发明技术有关的特权，从而激励创新[①]。

专利具有排他性，它赋予了发明者排除其他人实施该发明的权利。但因为获得专利必须满足许多条件，所以专利保护不可能适用于所有知识产权。因此，技术转移办公室需要寻求另一种形式的保护，使得技术转移办公室在研究过程的任何阶段都能保护成果或发明，且不限于寻求有创造性、低成本的保护机制。一些技术转移办公室的网站向访问者提供商业机密、商标和版权的介绍。我们认为，从许多方面来说，这一解决方案都非常有用。对于研究人员而言，他们将更了解保护其成果和创新的方法，鼓励他们向技术转移办公室披露其成果；对于技术转移办公室来说，这是促进其工作的方法之一，是出于公众利益开发、保护、转移和商业化研究成果。这就是为什么我们建议技术转移办公室的网站应该设置一些商业机密、商标和版权问题的介绍。

如前所述，专利是技术转移办公室采用的最常见的法律保护方法，而专利保护始于申请专利，但专利文件和申请专利的程序较为复杂。因此，在准备专利申请并将申请提交相关机构时，法律援助是可取且必要的。在必要的法律援助下，技术转移办公室可通过两种方式解决专利申请问题：一是与内部律师合作；二是与外部专利专家、律师或律师事务所合作。我们推荐第二种解决方案，因为它整合了在特定领域的最佳的专利专家，而且具有成本效益优势。专利申请可以由专家撰写，但在起草过程中，研究人员需要与专利专家一起工作。

专利申请准备完成后，提交到相关机构，且须遵循各个国家不同的程

①Costas, I., Euro, A., Echarri, J.M., Piqué, R. and Condom, P., 2012. From research to market: Key issues of technology transfer from public research centres to businesses. *Imprimeix SL*:18.

Accordingly, it is impossible to provide a step-by-step approach to these procedures. The process of patent protection results in issuance or abandonment. When talking about patents, researchers should be informed that the patents are territorial rights and patent protection is subject to each individual country's laws. Until now, there are no universal patent applications in all world countries. But, some regions (for example Europe, Africa) have regional patent offices①, and they have developed regional patent protection procedures. In regard to this, the international application under the Patent Cooperation Treaty (PCT) should be mentioned. The researchers should be aware of the fact that the patent process could last for years.

2.5 Commercialization

Commercialization is either through an established company, or sharing a license of the company, or through start-ups. Most of the universities only start to find licensees immediately after the patent is filed for the prior art.② Commercialization consists of a few sub-activities as described below.

2.5.1 Marketing patented technology

In commercialization, one of the most challenging tasks for TTOs is marketing patented inventions. A crucial point of this task is informal and formal networks with individuals and organizations. Experience has shown that a large number of successful licensing agreements result from contacts provided by the researchers/inventors themselves who are likely to know better than anybody else which companies might be interested in a given technology.③ Studies have shown that 70% of licensees were known to the inventors.④ This leads to the conclusion that researchers' involvement

---

① See: the European Patent Office (EPO) and the African Regional Intellectual Property Organization (ARIPO).

② Ismail, K., Omar, W.Z.W. and Majid, I.A., 2011. The commercialization process of patents by universities. *African Journal of Business Management*, 5(17):7201.

③ WIPO, 2007. *Technology transfer, intellectual property and effective university-industry partnerships: the experience of China, India, Japan, Philippines, the Republic of Korea, Singapore and Thailand*:45.

④ EST., 2019. *Best Practices on Technology Transfer Innovation Potential of EST*:6.

序。但由于这些程序的具体步骤无法提供，专利保护就会产生发放专利或放弃专利申请两个结果。研究人员须意识到，专利属于领土权利，专利保护受各国法律管辖。但目前为止，世界各国还没有普遍适用的专利保护程序，但是，一些地区（例如：欧洲、非洲）设有区域专利局[①]，并制定了区域专利保护程序。就此而言，可参考《专利合作条约》下的国际专利申请。因此，专利保护过程可能持续多年。

2.5 商业化

专利技术通过已成立公司、分公司或者是一家新的初创公司的许可，方可进行商业化。由于现有技术的原因，大多数大学在专利申请后就立即开始寻找被许可方[②]。如下文所述，商业化由几个次级活动组成。

2.5.1 营销专利技术

在商业化阶段，技术转移办公室最具挑战性的任务之一是营销专利发明。这项任务的关键在于与个人和组织建立非正式和正式的关系网。经验表明，大量成功的许可协议是由研究人员或发明者自己联系实现的，他们可能比任何人更了解公司对某一特定技术的兴趣[③]。研究表明，70%的许可持有人（被许可方）是与发明者相识的[④]。这就得出这样一个结论，在确定潜在的许可方和其他与行业或企业合作的机会时，研究人员

---

① See: the European Patent Office (EPO) and the African Regional Intellectual Property Organization (ARIPO).

② Ismail, K., Omar, W.Z.W. and Majid, I.A., 2011. The commercialization process of patents by universities. *African Journal of Business Management*, 5(17):7201.

③ WIPO, 2007. *Technology transfer, intellectual property and effective university - industry partnerships: the experience of China, India, Japan, Philippines, the Republic of Korea, Singapore and Thailand*:45.

④ EST., 2019. *Best Practices on Technology Transfer Innovation Potential of EST*:6.

and their collaboration with TTO are very important in identifying the prospective licensees and other opportunities for collaboration with the industry and businesses. On the other hand, TTOs consistently, methodically and broadly promote innovations that are patented and available for licensing, using a variety of sources and strategies like websites, catalogs, video demonstrations, technology exchanges, local, national and regional events, flyers, conferences and seminars, faculty publications and presentations, mail or direct personal contacts and face-to-face meetings. TTOs also use the initial contact of researchers for advertising inventions.

During this phase, TTOs recognize possible companies are prepared to involve time, money and people in bringing the innovation to market. It can take months and sometimes years to locate a potential licensee, depending on the attractiveness of the invention, its stage of development, competing technologies, and the market's needs.① But finding a potential licensee also depends on quality criteria about potential partners like how well they run their business, their capabilities and characteristics.②

Also, by providing this activity, TTOs find the most appropriate sources for the sale of innovation while protecting the university's intellectual property, and at the same time reduce uncertainty for firms.③

2.5.2 Negotiating licensing agreements

The university often owns the invention's intellectual property rights and can license the protected invention to a firm.④ The task of TTOs is to decide for the licensee with the best capability for commercialization of the invention. An invention can

---

① University of California, Berkeley, 2019. An Inventor's Guide Technology Transfer, Berkeley IPIRA Intellectual property & industry research alliances:20.

② See: U.S. Department of Energy Innovations and Innovation Program, 1989. Making Licensing Decision, Ratner and Prestia.

③ See: Etzkowitz, H., 2003. Innovation in innovation: The triple helix of university-industry-government relations. *Social science information*, 42(3):293–337.

④ Friedman and Silberman, 2003 cited in Samantha R. Bradley, Christopher S. Hayter, Albert N. Link, Models and Methods of University Technology Transfer Department of Economics Working Paper Series, The University of North Carolina Greensboro, 2013.

的参与及其与技术转移办公室的合作是非常重要的。另一方面，技术转移办公室通常可以使用各种资源和策略，如网站、目录、视频演示、技术交流，开展本地、国家和区域性活动，传单、会议和研讨会、教师的出版物和演讲、邮件或直接个人联系和面对面会议等方式，有序并广泛地推广已获得专利和许可证的创新，还能利用与研究人员的初步接触来宣传这些发明。

在这一阶段，技术转移办公室要能辨别潜在公司准备投入的时间、资金和人力资源。将创新推向市场可能需要几个月，甚至几年才能找到潜在的被许可方，这都取决于发明的吸引力、开发阶段、竞争技术和市场的需要①。但是，寻找潜在的被许可方也取决于潜在合作伙伴的质量标准，比如经营业务的水平、能力和特点②。

此外，通过提供这一营销措施，技术转移办公室找到了最合适的创新销售渠道，在此过程中，既保护了大学的知识产权，又减少了企业的不确定性③。

2.5.2 许可协议的谈判

一般来说，大学拥有某项发明的知识产权，并可以将受产权保护的发明授权给一家公司④。而技术转移办公室的任务是遴选具有能使该发明最佳商业化能力的被许可方。当然，一项发明可以授权给多个被许可方。

---

① University of California, Berkeley, 2019. An Inventor' s Guide Technology Transfer, Berkeley IPIRA Intellectual property & industry research alliances:20.

② See: U.S. Department of Energy Innovations and Innovation Program, 1989. Making Licensing Decision, Ratner and Prestia.

③See: Etzkowitz, H., 2003. Innovation in innovation: The triple helix of university-industry-government relations. *Social science information*, 42(3):293–337.

④ Friedman and Silberman, 2003 cited in Samantha R. Bradley, Christopher S. Hayter, Albert N. Link, Models and Methods of University Technology Transfer Department of Economics Working Paper Series, The University of North Carolina Greensboro, 2013.

be licensed to multiple licensees.

Licensing agreement is a legal contract where the licensor grants and the licensee acquire the right to use thelicensor's technology in specified terms and conditions.[①] Respectively, it needs legal knowledge. But, the conclusion of the licensing agreement is also connected with negotiating and, at the same time, needs other types of skills besides legal knowledge. Namely, negotiating is an essential part of the process of reaching a licensing agreement, but it is influenced by emotions, too, not only by knowledge. It requires skill to reach a compromise because this "discussion" ends with a mutually acceptable solution.

The practice shows that the best time for negotiating licensing agreements is before the research is complete and before its market price is obvious; therefore, negotiating in this phase is in the best interest of both parties. TTO negotiates licensing agreements on behalf of the researcher. But the licensor and licensee must be acquainted with the fact that the negotiation seeks a"win-win" solution and its aim is to find an original long-term solution for the benefit of both parties.

Negotiating a license agreement is a separate process with its different phases.[②]

2.5.3 License

A license is an agreement where the IP owner grants another party permission to assume the IP's rights and authorizes the licensee to use the invention. License agreements describe the rights and responsibilities related to the use and exploitation of intellectual property developed at the university.[③] A primary licensing decision is whether to license exclusively or non-exclusively. An exclusive license means that no person or company other than the named licensee can exploit the relevant intellec-

① See: World Intellectual Property Organization, International Trade Centre., 2010. *Exchanging Value: Negotiating Technology Licensing Agreements a Training Manual*: 82.

② Ibid.

③ See: American University of Beirut, Office of Grants and Contracts, available at https://website.aub.edu.lb/ogc/technology/Pages/TTU%20Guide.aspx#9, accessed 22 September 2020; University of California, Berkeley, 2019. *An Inventor's Guide Technology Transfer*. Berkeley IPIRA Intellectual Property & Industry Research Alliances: 20.

许可协议属于法律合同，许可方授予被许可方获得在特定条款和情况下使用许可方技术的权利[①]，双方都应具备一定的法律知识。但是，缔结许可协议也与谈判有关，除法律知识外，还需要其他类型的技能。也就是说，谈判是达成许可协议过程中必不可少的一部分，但它也受到其他因素的影响。谈判不仅受知识的影响，还需要一定的技巧才能达成，因为这种“讨论”是以互相都接受的解决方案结束的。

实践表明，谈判许可协议的最佳时间是在研究完成之前，同时在其市场价格明显之前，因此，在这一阶段进行谈判，符合双方的最佳利益。技术转移办公室代表研究人员谈判许可协议。但是，许可方和被许可方必须认识到，谈判寻求的是一种“双赢”的解决方案，其目的是找到最初有利于双方的长期解决方案。

许可协议的谈判是一个单独的过程，具有不同的阶段[②]。

2.5.3 许可证

许可证是一种协议，知识产权所有者授予另一方许可，使其取得知识产权，并授权被许可方使用本发明的权利。许可协议规定了与大学知识产权的使用和开发相关的权利和责任[③]。许可证主要决定的是独家许可还是

① See: World Intellectual Property Organization, International Trade Centre., 2010. *Exchanging Value: Negotiating Technology Licensing Agreements a Training Manual*:82.

② Ibid.

③ See: American University of Beirut, Office of Grants and Contracts, available at https://website.aub.edu.lb/ogc/technology/Pages/TTU%20Guide.aspx#9, accessed 22 September 2020; University of California, Berkeley, 2019. *An Inventor's Guide Technology Transfer*. Berkeley IPIRA Intellectual Property & Industry Research Alliances:20.

tual property rights.[①] A non-exclusive license grants the licensee the right to use the intellectual property, but means that the licensor remains free to exploit the same intellectual property and to allow other licensees to also exploit the same intellectual property.[②] Firms typically desire exclusive licenses to maintain proprietary control of the technology, but non-exclusive licenses can be granted as well, depending on scope, sector, or geography.[③] TTO practice shows that TTOs should consider granting exclusive licenses to inventions that require significant investment to reach the market or are so embryonic that exclusivity is necessary to induce the investment needed to develop and commercialize the invention.[④] University license agreements usually stipulate that the licensee should diligently seek to bring the intellectual property into commercial use for the public good and provide a reasonable return to the university.[⑤]

2.5.4 A start-up or a spinoff company

Under certain circumstances, the best choice for commercializing innovation is the creation of a new company. In these situations, innovation can be commercialized through a new start-up or spinoff company. This new company has an obligation to develop, market, and sell the invention. The main difference between start-ups

---

① See: Association of University Technology Managers, 2007. In the public interest: nine points to consider in licensing university technology.

② See: U.S. Naval Research Laboratory, Technology Transfer Office available at https://www.nrl.navy.mil/techtransfer/FAQs/licensing#types, accessed 22 September 2020.

③ See: Van Norman, G.A. and Eisenkot, R., 2017. Technology transfer: from the research bench to commercialization: part 2: the commercialization process. *JACC: Basic to Translational Science*, 2(2): 197–208; Siegel, D.S., Waldman, D.A., Atwater, L.E. and Link, A.N., 2003. Commercial knowledge transfers from universities to firms: improving the effectiveness of university-industry collaboration. *The Journal of High Technology Management Research*, 14(1): 111–133; Bercovitz, J. and Feldman, M., 2006. Entrepreneurial universities and technology transfer: A conceptual framework for understanding knowledge-based economic development. *The Journal of Technology Transfer*, 31(1): 175–188.

④ University of California, Office of Technology Transfer, 2012. University Licensing Guidelines: 4.

⑤ See: Stanford University Office of Technology Licensing, 2019. Inventor's Guide.

非独家许可[①]。独家许可是指除指定被许可方以外的任何人或公司不能利用相关的知识产权。非独家许可授予被许可方使用知识产权的权利，但意味着许可方仍然可以自由地利用同一知识产权，并允许任何其他被许可方也利用同一知识产权[②]。企业通常希望获得独家许可证，以保持对技术的专有控制，但非独家许可证的授予也取决于范围、部门或地理情况[③]。技术转移办公室的实践表明，技术转移办公室应该考虑对那些需要大量投资才能进入市场，或者开发处于萌芽阶段，有必要通过独家许可降低发明开发和商业化成本的发明授予独家许可[④]。大学许可协议通常规定，被许可方应努力寻求将知识产权用于商业用途，以促进公共利益，并向大学提供合理的回报[⑤]。

2.5.4 初创公司或分公司

有时，创新商业化的最佳选择是创建新公司。一项创新可以通过一家新的初创或分公司商业化，这家新公司有义务开发、推广和销售发明。

---

①See：Association of University Technology Managers，2007. In the public interest：nine points to conser in licensing university technology.

②See：U.S. Naval Research Labaratory，Technology Transfer Office available at https://www.nrl.navy.mil/techtransfer/FAQs/licensing#types，accessed 22 September 2020.

③ See：Van Norman，G.A. and Eisenkot，R.，2017. Technology transfer：from the research bench to commercialization：part 2：the commercialization process. *JACC：Basic to Translational Science*，2(2)：197–208；Siegel，D.S.，Waldman，D.A.，Atwater，L.E. and Link，A.N.，2003. Commercial knowledge transfers from universities to firms：improving the effectiveness of university-industry collaboration. *The Journal of High Technology Management Research*，14(1)：111–133；Bercovitz，J. and Feldman，M.，2006. Entrepreneurial universities and technology transfer：A conceptual framework for understanding knowledge-based economic development. *The Journal of Technology Transfer*，31(1)：175–188.

④University of California，Office of Technology Transfer，2012. University Licensing Guidelines：4.

⑤ See：Stanford University Office of Technology Licensing，2019. Inventor's Guide.

and spinoffs is that spinoffs are created inside the mother-institution, but their main goal is the same: commercialization ofuniversities' innovations.

The choice to establish a new company for commercializing invention may be made by the inventor(s) or other entities/entrepreneurs.① The choice to establish a new company relates to the question: "When starting a new company is the best choice". According to Lowe (2002), starting a new company is the best choice when academic entrepreneurs cannot license their technology to large companies or external entrepreneurs.② But TTOs state that they encourage start-ups due to the following reasons:③

• Start-ups and universities have the same public mission, i.e., they serve for the good and benefit of the society;

• Successful start-up means help for the universities in regard to the employment of high-quality academic staff;

• Start-ups increase local economic development and create jobs, and thus present worth of university research to the society;

• In some cases, start-ups are the only alternative because individual innovations cannot be licensed, and the commercialization of invention needs great work;

• Start-ups make money for the inventor, the university, and the business and investment community simply because sometimes no big companies recognize the invention's value.④

Some TTOs give preference to the inventor's wish and passion if that individual

① Berkeley Office of Intellectual Property and Industry Research Alliance. 2015. *An Inventor's Guide Technology Transfer at the University of California*: 23.

② Lowe R. 2002. Invention, innovation and entrepreneurship: the commercialization of university research by inventor-founded firms. PhD dissertation, University of California at Berkeley.

③ See: University of Colorado, venture Partners at CU Boulder, available at https://www.colorado. edu/techtransfer/investigators/transferring - your - innovation/starting - compa ny#why_does_cu_ encourage_ startups_-167 accessed 20 September 2020; University of South Florida, USF Research & Innovation, available at https://www.usf.edu/research - innovation/pl/for - entrepreneurs. aspx, accessed 20 September 2020.

④ See: Fisher, L.M., 1998. The innovation incubator: Technology transfer at Stanford University. *Strategy and Business*, 76-86.

初创公司和分公司的主要区别在于，分公司是在母体机构内创造的，但它们的主要目标都是大学创新的商业化。

发明人或其他实体/企业家可以选择设立一家新的发明商业化公司[①]。而成立一家新公司的选择涉及这样一个问题，即："创办一家新公司是不是最好的选择?"当学术型创业者无法将他们的技术授权给大公司或外部企业家时，创办一家新公司是最好的选择[②]。技术转移办公室则鼓励初创企业，原因如下[③]：

• 初创企业和大学有相同的公共使命，即：为社会的利益服务；

• 成功的初创企业意味着能够帮助大学高质量的学术人员就业；

• 初创企业能促进当地的经济发展，创造就业机会，从而为社会展示大学研究的价值；

• 在某些情况下，因为个人创新不能获得许可，而发明的商业化需要大量的工作，初创企业是唯一的选择；

• 初创企业为发明者、大学、企业和投资团体谋取利益仅仅是因为，有时没有大公司认识到发明的价值[④]。

如果发明者想创办一家公司，技术转移办公室应优先考虑发明者的愿

① Berkeley Office of Intellectual Property and Industry Research Alliance. 2015. *An Inventor's Guide Technology Transfer at the University of California*: 23.

② Lowe R. 2002. Invention, innovation and entrepreneurship: the commercialization of university research by inventor-founded firms. PhD dissertation, University of California at Berkeley.

③ See: University of Colorado, venture Partners at CU Boulder, available at https://www.colorado.edu/techtransfer/investigators/transferring - your - innovation/starting - compa ny#why_does_cu_ encourage_ startups_-167 accessed 20 September 2020; University of South Florida, USF Research & Innovation, available at https://www.usf.edu/research - innovation/pl/for - entrepreneurs.aspx, accessed 20 September 2020.

④See: Fisher, L.M., 1998. The innovation incubator: Technology transfer at Stanford University. *Strategy and Business*: 76–86.

wants to start a company.

Starting a new company faces different types of challenges. Therefore, when deciding to start and operate a new company, at least a few crucial factors should be taken into consideration. In relation to creating a new start-up, most of the universities enumerate the following crucial factors:[①]

- Development risk (often companies are unwilling to take the risk of unproven technology);
- Development costs versus investment return (can the investors obtain expected rates of return?);
- Potential for multiple products or services from the same technology;
- Sufficiently large competitive advantage and the target market;
- Potential revenues are sufficient to sustain and grow a company.

The commercialization of the innovation through a new company involves TTO, too. In these cases, TTOs are involved during the whole process: starting from the decision for this path of commercialization, through the establishment of the new company, patenting and licensing the invention, even working together with the new company.

In regard to the previous analysis, it should be noted that the processes of marketing the invention, acquiring IP protection, and negotiating licensing agreements and financial returns do not necessarily follow a linear path, and these processes can occur simultaneously.[②]

---

① Penn State University, 2019. An Inventor's Guide to Technology Transfer: 24; University of Toronto, Innovations & Partnerships Office, 2018. Inventor's Guide to Technology Transfer: 27.

② Leyden, D.P. and Link, A.N., 2015. *Public sector entrepreneurship: US technology and innovation policy*. Oxford University Press, USA: 107.

望和热情。

创办一家新公司面临着不同类型的挑战。因此，在决定创办和经营一家新公司时，大多数大学列举了以下应考虑的关键因素[①]：

- 发展风险（公司往往不愿意为未经证实的技术承担风险）；
- 开发成本与投资回报（投资者能否获得预期回报率）；
- 同一技术的多个产品或服务的潜在多样性；
- 足够大的竞争优势和目标市场；
- 足以维持和发展一家公司的潜在收入。

通过一家新公司实现创新的商业化也涉及技术转移办公室的工作。技术转移办公室贯穿在决定开始商业化，通过建立新公司，为发明申请专利和许可，甚至与新公司合作的整个过程中。

上述分析指出，销售发明、获得知识产权保护、谈判许可协议和资金回报的过程不一定遵循线性路径，这些过程可以同时发生[②]。

① Penn State University, 2019. An Inventor's Guide to Technology Transfer: 24; University of Toronto, Innovations & Partnerships Office, 2018. Inventor's Guide to Technology Transfer: 27.

②Leyden, D.P. and Link, A.N., 2015. *Public sector entrepreneurship: US technology and innovation policy*. Oxford University Press, USA: 107.

3 WHY TECHNOLOGY TRANSFER OFFICE?

TTO offers, produces and develops numerous benefits for the inventors, research organizations, businesses, as well as for the society and region. Numerous studies express TTO's abilities.[①] TTO's benefits are causally related to its activities. The analysis of TTO's activities points to the critical benefits as described below.

3.1 Benefits of TTO

3.1.1 TTO's impact on the economy

One of the biggest benefits of TTO is its impact on the economy. Well-

① See: George, G., 2005. Learning to be capable: patenting and licensing at the Wisconsin Alumni Research Foundation 1925–2002. *Industrial and corporate change*, 14(1): 119–151; Lockett, A. and Wright, M., 2005. Resources, capabilities, risk capital and the creation of university spin-out companies. *Research policy*, 34(7): 1043–1057; Markman, G.D., Gianiodis, P. T., Phan, P.H. and Balkin, D.B., 2005. Innovation speed: Transferring university technology to market. *Research policy*, 34(7): 1058–1075; Rasmussen, E. and Borch, O.J., 2010. University capabilities in facilitating entrepreneurship: A longitudinal study of spinoff ventures at mid-range universities. *Research policy*, 39(5): 602–612; Alexander, A.T. and Martin, D.P., 2013. Intermediaries for open innovation: A competence-based comparison of knowledge transfer offices practices. *Technological Forecasting and Social Change*, 80(1): 38–49.

第三章 技术转移办公室的意义

许多研究都证明了技术转移办公室的能力。技术转移办公室为发明者、研究机构、企业以及社会和地区的生产和开发提供服务[①]。而技术转移办公室的优势与其开展的活动有因果关系。因此，对技术转移办公室活动的分析得出了其主要优势，如下所述。

3.1 技术转移办公室的作用

3.1.1 技术转移办公室对经济的影响

技术转移办公室最大的作用之一是对经济的影响。大学和企业之间良

① See：George，G.，2005. Learning to be capable：patenting and licensing at the Wisconsin Alumni Research Foundation 1925–2002. *Industrial and corporate change*，14(1)：119–151；Lockett，A. and Wright，M.，2005. Resources，capabilities，risk capital and the creation of university spin-out companies. *Research policy*，34(7)：1043–1057；Markman，G.D.，Gianiodis，P. T.，Phan，P.H. and Balkin，D.B.，2005. Innovation speed：Transferring university technology to market. *Research policy*，34(7)：1058–1075；Rasmussen，E. and Borch，O.J.，2010. University capabilities in facilitating entrepreneurship：A longitudinal study of spinoff ventures at mid-range universities. *Research policy*，39(5)：602–612；Alexander，A.T. and Martin，D.P.，2013. Intermediaries for open innovation：A competence-based comparison of knowledge transfer offices practices. *Technological Forecasting and Social Change*，80(1)：38–49.

functionong links between universities and firms can stimulate economic growth.①
Economists have agreed for decades that a large component of modern economic growth has to be driven by "innovation", that is, the arrival of new ideas and technologies.②

According to the AUTM 2018 survey③, academic research is fueling impressive economic gains: 1,080 start-ups were formed in 2018, making a direct impact on local economies, with more than 69 percent of the new businesses remaining in their institution's home state; 7,625 USA patents were issued in 2018, the most ever reported in the survey, as research institutions invest and protect intellectual property arising from academic research and consumers and businesses benefited from 7,947 new products created over the past decade. The impact of technology transfer on the US economy has been enormous: technology transfer has contributed $518 billion on the USA gross domestic product and $1.1 trillion on the US gross industrial output from 1996–2013. The impact of that has produced 3.8 million jobs for the USA economy.④

The AUTM and UNICO have disseminated data and case studies of how the technology and knowledge transfers can benefit society, emphasizing that these positive economic effects indirectly influence research organizations - business partnerships, culture change and the well-being of society.⑤ We agree with Campbell that these long-term returns supplement shorter-term, more tangible returns such as in-

① E. MansfieldAcademic research and industrial innovations Res. Policy, 20 (1991): 1–12 cited in Dagmara Weckowska, Learning in university technology transfer offices: transactions-focused and relations-focused approaches to commercialization of academic research, Technovation Volumes 41–42, July–August 2015: 62–74.

② Macilwain, C., 2010. Science economics: What science is really worth. *Nature*, 465 (7299): 682–684.

③ Available at https://autm.net/surveys-and-tools/surveys/licensing-survey/2018-licensing-activity-survey, accessed 23 September 2020.

④ Nag, D., 2017. The changing face of university technology transfer. *IPWatchdog*.

⑤ Campbell, A.F., 2007. How to set up a technology transfer office: experiences from Europe. *Intellectual Property Management in Health and Agricultural Innovation: A handbook of best practices*: 559–566.

好的运作关系可以刺激经济增长①。经济学家一致认为，现代经济增长的一大部分必须由“创新”驱动，即新思想和新技术的发展②。

值得注意的是，技术转移办公室对经济的影响也得到了政治家们的承认，这在很大程度上取决于政治背景，即国家战略。③比如，美国大学技术管理人员协会（AUTM）2018年的一项调查表明，学术研究可以产生显著的经济效益。2018年，1080家初创企业在美国成立，都对当地经济产生了直接影响，其中超过69%的新企业仍留在其所在州。2018年，美国颁发了7625项专利，这是调查中报告数量最多的一次，原因在于研究机构投资并保护学术研究产生的知识产权，而消费者和企业也受益于过去十年创造的7947种新产品。技术转移对美国经济的影响是巨大的。从1996年至2013年，技术转移对美国国内生产总值贡献了1580亿美元，对美国工业总产值贡献了11000亿美元，也为美国创造了380万个就业机会④。

美国大学技术管理人员协会和大学企业协会（UNICO）展示了关于技术和知识转移如何造福社会的数据和案例研究，强调这些积极的经济影响也间接影响研究组织—商业伙伴关系、文化变革和社会福祉⑤。我们也认为，这些长期回报补充了短期的真实回报，如收入、获得的资源和专门知

① E. MansfieldAcademic research and industrial innovations Res. Policy, 20 (1991): 1–12 cited in Dagmara Weckowska, Learning in university technology transfer offices: transactions-focused and relations-focused approaches to commercialization of academic research, Technovation Volumes 41–42, July–August 2015: 62–74.

② Macilwain, C., 2010. Science economics: What science is really worth. *Nature*, 465 (7299): 682–684.

③ Available at https://autm.net/surveys-and-tools/surveys/licensing-survey/2018-licensing-activity-survey, accessed 23 September 2020.

④ Nag, D., 2017. The changing face of university technology transfer. *IPWatchdog*.

⑤ Campbell, A.F., 2007. How to set up a technology transfer office: experiences from Europe. *Intellectual Property Management in Health and Agricultural Innovation: A handbook of best practices*: 559–566.

come, access to resources and expertise, and program delivery.[①]

3.1.2 Impact of professional technicians on technology transformation

As previously mentioned, TTO comes in a variety of structures, but its goal is always the same: implementation of technology transfer process in the best interest of the innovator, research organization and society. Implementation of technology transfer process is, without exception, connected with laws, by-laws, institutional regulations and other regulators' requirements which may differ from state to state as well as international legislation. Technology transfer process starts with the innovation disclosure, which means a written description of the invention that is provided to TTO and evaluation of the size and growth of the potential market on the basic level. Then the process continues with the commercialization of the innovation, which means protecting innovations through trade secrets, trademarks, copyrights or patents; marketing of protected technology; negotiating licensing agreements; making a decision for licensing agreement or establishing a new company for commercializing IP rights and a lot of sub-question crucial for the successful TTO. Santoro, M.D. and Bierly, P.E. (2006) find that social connectedness, trust, university-research centers, technology transfer and intellectual property policies, technological relatedness and technological capability are significant facilitators of knowledge transfer.[②] Actually, this system requires researchers to have specific knowledge in order to act effectively and profitably. Debackere, K. and Veugelers, R. (2005) argue that among other critical elements in fostering an "effective" commercialization of the academic science base is implementing the appropriate decision and monitoring processes within the TTO.[③] Thus, it is easy to conclude that technology transfer process in all its stages asks for the design of appropriate decisions: starting from phone calls, through frequently and appropriate agreement editing, ending with concluded

① Ibid.

② Santoro, M.D. and Bierly, P.E., 2006. Facilitators of knowledge transfer in university-industry collaborations: A knowledge-based perspective. *IEEE Transactions on Engineering management*, 53(4):495–507.

③ See: Debackere, K. and Veugelers, R., 2005. The role of academic technology transfer organizations in improving industry science links. *Research policy*, 34(3):321–342.

识以及项目交付[①]。

3.1.2 技术转移对专业人员的要求

如前所述，技术转移办公室有多种结构，但其目标是相同的，就是以创新者、研究组织和社会的最佳利益来实施技术转移。

技术转移过程的实施毫无例外地与法律、规章制度、体制条例和其他具体的监管要求有关，这些要求可能因国家而异，也可能因国际立法而有所不同。技术转移过程从发明披露开始，在基本层面上，发明披露意味着向技术转移办公室提供对发明的书面描述材料，在材料中评估其潜在市场的规模和增长。这样，创新的商业化进程才能继续下去，这其中涉及商业秘密、商标、版权或专利保护创新，受保护技术的营销，谈判许可协议，就许可协议做出决定，或成立一家新的公司，将知识产权商业化，以及对成功的技术转移至关重要的许多小问题。社会联系、信任、大学研究中心、技术转移和知识产权政策、技术关联和技术能力是促进知识转移的重要因素[②]。事实上，这个系统需要研究人员有特定的知识才能产生效果并有利可图。促进学术科学基础“有效”商业化的另一关键要素是在技术转移办公室内实施适当的决策和监测程序[③]。因此，我们很容易得出结论，技术转移的所有阶段都要求做出适当的决定，从电话通话开始，通过频繁和适当的协议修订，最后缔结强制性协议。此外，技术转移过程必须全程监测，尤其监测其效率，因为它是通过成本和时间来衡量的。

---

① Ibid.

② Santoro, M.D. and Bierly, P.E., 2006. Facilitators of knowledge transfer in university-industry collaborations: A knowledge-based perspective. *IEEE Transactions on Engineering management*, 53(4):495-507.

③ See: Debackere, K. and Veugelers, R., 2005. The role of academic technology transfer organizations in improving industry science links. *Research policy*, 34(3):321-342.

obligatory agreements. Moreover, technology transfer process must be monitored all the way, especially its efficiency, because it is valued through money and time spent.

Swamidass, P.M. and Vulasa, V. (2009) see a considerable role of adequately trained staff and inventions processing capacity in TTO in the rate of commercialization of university inventions,[①] and this rate has positive impacts on university aspects (such as income and reputation). TTO has qualified and experienced staff always available for discussion, advice and assessment, assistance in intellectual property protection, sufficient technical capacity, as well as knowledge capacity in documents, and all of this in a timely and transparent manner.

3.1.3 Impact of technology transfer on research by technical professionals

TTO acts as a service center to the university, faculty, staff and students in all areas related to technology transfer, especially intellectual property, including providing seminars and consulting services as required.[②] The university with a TTO will have a higher expected number of patents than the university without a TTO, and the effect of the TTO increases over time.[③] We believe this influences theuniversity's reputation and public trust in the university.

Gulbrandsen, M. and Smeby, J.C.(2005) find that there is a significant relationship between industry funding and research performance: professors with industrial funding describe their research as applied to a greater extent, they collaborate more with other researchers both in academia and in industry, and they report more

---

① See: Swamidass, P.M. and Vulasa, V., 2009. Why university inventions rarely produce income? Bottlenecks in university technology transfer. *The Journal of technology transfer*, 34(4): 343-363.

② See University of Pretoria, 2019. Contracts and Innovation Office, available at https://www.up.ac.za/contracts-innovation-office/article/262155/innovation-technology-transfer, accessed 23 September 2020.

③ Bradley, S., Hayter, C.S. and Link, A., 2013. Models and methods of university technology transfer. *Foundations and trends in Entrepreneurship*, 9(6).

在技术转移办公室中，专业的工作人员及其对发明的处理能力，对大学发明的商业化率起着相当大的作用[①]，并且这一比率对大学的收入、声誉等方面都产生了积极影响。技术转移办公室有合适的经验丰富的专业人员，随时可提供讨论、咨询和评估及知识产权保护方面的援助，他们有足够的技术能力以及知识能力处理文件，所用方法都是及时和透明的。

3.1.3 技术转移对研究人员的影响

技术转移办公室作为大学、教职员工和学生的服务中心，负责与技术转移，特别是知识产权相关的所有领域，包括根据要求提供研讨会和咨询服务[②]。拥有技术转移办公室的大学将比没有技术转移办公室的大学拥有更多的专利数量，并且技术转移办公室的影响会随着时间的推移而增加[③]，同时也会对大学的声誉和公信力产生影响。

产业资助与研究绩效之间存在着显著的关系：拥有产业资助的教授所拥有的研究更容易被应用，他们与学术界和业界的其他研究人员合作更

① See: Swam ass, P.M. and Vulasa, V., 2009. Why university inventions rarely produce income? Bottlenecks in university technology transfer. *The Journal of technology transfer*, 34(4): 343-363.

② See University of Pretoria, 2019. Contracts and Innovation Office, available at https://www. up. ac. za/contracts - innovation - office/article/262155/innovation - technology - transfer, accessed 23 September 2020.

③ Bradley, S., Hayter, C.S. and Link, A., 2013. Models and methods of university technology transfer. *Foundations and trends in Entrepreneurship*, 9(6).

scientific publications as well as more frequent entrepreneurial results.① The ways in which TTO manages the technology transfer process encourage the growth of the researchers' successes because researchers become aware of the utilization and financial outcomes of their research and are free of unnecessary pressure. The university research community has always been under various forms of outside pressure—political, economic, and institutional—that have had the potential to impact, for better or worse, the nature and direction of academic research.② University researchers have long been exposed to a wide range of influences.③ Therefore, this TTO-researcher connection seems to be successful, stimulus and supportive for both researchers and universities.

TTO provides assistance in applying for programs supporting innovation.④ TTO, also, through its activities, generates interest and investment in emerging areas of research, with consequent gains or improvements in research funding.⑤

All previously described is actually benefited from university's work for society and a path of university's serving to the community.

3.1.4 Impact of technology transfer on the commercialization of inventions

TTO activities encourage broad practical applications of inventions which are directly connected to the private sector, industry, firms. This TTO's role showed as very important because successful innovation transfers from research to product faces

---

① See: Gulbrandsen, M. and Smeby, J.C., 2005. Industry funding and university professors' research performance. *Research policy*, 34(6):932-950.

② Caulfield, T. and Ogbogu, U., 2015. The commercialization of university-based research: Balancing risks and benefits. *BMC medical ethics*, 16(1):1.

③ Caulfield, T., 2012. Should scientists have to always show the commercial benefits of their research?available at https://policyoptions.irpp.org/magazines/talking-science/caulfield/, accessed 23 September 2020.

④ See: DISA. 2020. Technology Transfer Program. Available at https://www.disa.mil/About/CTO/Technology_Transfer_Program

⑤ Caulfield, T. and Ogbogu, U., 2015. The commercialization of university-based research: Balancing risks and benefits. *BMC medical ethics*, 16(1):3.

多，更频繁地出版和发表科研和创新成果[①]。技术转移办公室管理技术转移过程的方式促进了研究人员的成功，因为研究人员已经意识到其研究的使用效果和经济效益，并且不会产生不必要的压力。大学研究机构一直承受着各种形式的外部压力——政治、经济和体制[②]，而这些压力已经有可能影响学术研究的性质和方向，无论是好是坏，长期以来，大学研究人员都受到了广泛的影响[③]。因此，这种技术转移办公室与研究人员之间的联系似乎是成功的，能够刺激和支持研究人员和大学。

技术转移办公室能协助申请支持创新的方案[④]，还通过其工作，激发投资者对新研究领域的兴趣，吸引投资，从而增加或提高研究资金[⑤]。

上述内容实际上都受益于大学为社会所做的工作以及大学为社会服务的方式。

3.1.4 技术转移对发明商业化的影响

技术转移办公室的活动鼓励了直接与私营企业、产业和公司有关的

① See: Gulbrandsen, M. and Smeby, J.C., 2005. Industry funding and university professors' research performance. *Research policy*, 34(6):932-950.

② Caulfield, T. and Ogbogu, U., 2015. The commercialization of university-based research: Balancing risks and benefits. *BMC medical ethics*, 16(1):1.

③ Caulfield, T., 2012. Should scientists have to always show the commercial benefits of their research? available at https://policyoptions.irpp.org/magazines/talking - science/caulfield/, accessed 23 September 2020.

④ See: DISA. 2020. "Technology Transfer Program". Available at https://www.disa.mil/About/CTO/Technology_Transfer_Program

⑤ Caulfield, T. and Ogbogu, U., 2015. The commercialization of university-based research: Balancing risks and benefits. *BMC medical ethics*, 16(1):3.

numerous obstacles[①]: diverse perspectives on the desired outputs, culture clashes, bureaucratic inflexibility, poorly designed reward systems, and ineffective management. TTOs are designed to bring together a range of aspects of this collaboration. A complete list of all objectives and types of collaborations cannot be listed exhaustively.[②] However, the most important reasons for entering a collaboration are: complementing competence, knowledge and technologies to advance research and development; obtaining access to resources that are available only from specific partners (e.g., clinical research); broadening the scope of the innovation process; exploiting existing IP through the inclusion of specific competence; attaining critical mass to address complex projects.[③]

Cohen, Guest, and Latham (2008) believe that researchers can and should do more to educate practitioners about research findings and processes.[④] As Rynes, S.L. (2007) notes, research needs to be done to determine: a. why practitioners don't believe some of the researchers' findings, b. why they do not implement them, even if they believe them.[⑤] In our view, TTOs, through technology transfer process, make strong contributions exactly to this request. Namely, promotion of public availability of innovations, promotion of collaboration between the industry and research institutions and finding ways for its increase as well as facilitation of their relationship are TTOs main tasks.

Siegel, D., Wright, M., Chapple, W. and Lockett, A. (2008) argue that TTOs play a critical role in the diffusion of innovation and the development of new

---

① See: Siegel, D.S., Waldman, D.A., Atwater, L.E. and Link, A.N., 2003. Commercial knowledge transfers from universities to firms: improving the effectiveness of university-industry collaboration. *The Journal of High Technology Management Research*, 14(1): 111–133.

② Abuja, P., Carapina, T., Kort, De M., Raess, M., Tieken C. and Wagstaff N. 2019. *Academia-Industry Collaboration Best Practices Guide*. Corbel: 5.

③ Ibid.

④ Rynes, S.L., 2007. Editor's afterword: Let's create a tipping point: What academics and practitioners can do, alone and together. *Academy of Management Journal*, 50(5): 1050.

⑤ Ibid.

发明的商业化应用。从研究到产品的成功创新转移面临许多障碍[①]，如：对预期产出的不同看法、文化冲突、官僚机构的僵化、设计不良的奖励制度和无效的管理，因此，技术转移办公室对发明商业化的作用十分关键。技术转移办公室旨在克服各种障碍，整合多方资源进行合作[②]。开展合作的主要原因包括补充能力、知识和技术的缺陷，以推动研究和发展；只能从特定合作伙伴获得资源（例如：临床研究领域）；扩大创新过程的范围；通过现有的特定能力来利用现有的知识产权；达到临界规模以解决复杂的项目[③]。

研究人员可以且应该做更多的工作来帮助从业者了解研究结果和过程[④]。正如一些学者所指出的，需要通过研究来确定：（1）为什么从业者不相信一些研究人员的发现？（2）即使从业者相信研究人员，为什么从业者不实施研究人员的发现[⑤]？技术转移办公室对从业者了解研究结果和过程做出了极大的贡献，促进了创新的商业化。因此，促进行业和研究机构之间的合作，寻找增加创新的途径以及促进它们之间的关系是技术转移办公室的主要任务。

技术转移办公室在创新的商业化和新技术基础设施的发展中起着至

① See: Siegel, D.S., Waldman, D.A., Atwater, L.E. and Link, A.N., 2003. Commercial knowledge transfers from universities to firms: improving the effectiveness of university industry collaboration. *The Journal of High Technology Management Research*, 14(1):111-133.

② Abuja, P., Carapina, T., Kort, De M., Raess, M., Tieken C. and Wagstaff N. 2019. *Academia-Industry Collaboration Best Practices Guide*. Corbel:5.

③ Ibid.

④ Rynes, S.L., 2007. Editor's afterword: Let's create a tipping point: What academics and practitioners can do, alone and together. *Academy of Management Journal*, 50(5):1050

⑤ Ibid.

technology infrastructure.[①] Siegel, D., Wright, M., Chapple, W. and Lockett, A.[②] suggest that increased licensing is due primarily to an increased willingness of faculty and administrators to license and increased business reliance on external research and development rather than a shift in faculty research.[③] Respectively, trust is a very important link for boosting research organizations-firms partnership. TTO ensures that all the participants: research organization, researcher and businesses obtain sufficient rights and monetary benefits. Additionally, experienced and professional TTO staff minimizes the technology transfer process's cost and maximizes its profits.

3.2 Risks and bridges to successful operation of TTO

TTOs face risks on the way to achieving their vision. This section describes key risks and bridges to successful operation of TTO.

3.2.1 Financial questions

Financial risks relate to businesses, research organizations as well as to TTOs play a critical role in the technology transfer process. During technology transfer processes, the private sector deals with money losses and opportunity costs. Private-sector money is needed to both fund and translate research into applications.[④] Without the industry involvement, many of the potentially beneficial basic science discover-

① See: Siegel, D., Wright, M., Chapple, W. and Lockett, A., 2008. Assessing the relative performance of university technology transfer in the US and UK: A stochastic distance function approach. *Econ. Innov. New Techn.*, 17(7-8):717-729.

② See: Siegel, D., Wright, M., Chapple, W. and Lockett, A., 2008. Assessing the relative performance of university technology transfer in the US and UK: A stochastic distance function approach. *Econ. Innov. New Techn.*, 17(7-8):717-729.

③ See: Siegel, D., Wright, M., Chapple, W. and Lockett, A., 2008. Assessing the relative performance of university technology transfer in the US and UK: A stochastic distance function approach. *Econ. Innov. New Techn.*, 17(7-8):717-729.

④ Caulfield, T., 2012. Should scientists have to always show the commercial benefits of their research? Available at https://policyoptions.irpp.org/magazines/talking-science/caulfield/, accessed 23 September 2020.

关重要的作用[①]。许可的增加主要由于大学教师和管理人员对许可的意愿提升[②]，以及企业对外部研发的依赖性增加，而不是由于教师研究的转变[③]。信任是促进研究机构与企业合作的重要环节。技术转移办公室要确保所有参与者，包括研究机构、研究人员和企业，都能获得足够的权利和经济利益。此外，经验丰富和专业的技术转移办公室工作人员能够尽可能地减少技术转移的成本，并最大限度地发挥其务实的特点。

3.2 技术转移办公室面临的风险

技术转移办公室在运作过程中会面临诸多风险，本节将总结归纳技术转移办公室须化解的风险。

3.2.1 财务风险

涉及企业、研究组织以及技术转移组织的财务风险，在技术转移过程中影响重大。在技术转移过程中，私营企业处理资金损失和机会成本，使用资金来资助研究并将其转化为应用[④]。如果没有相关产业的参与，许多

---

① See: Siegel, D., Wright, M., Chapple, W. and Lockett, A., 2008. Assessing the relative performance of university technology transfer in the US and UK: A stochastic distance function approach. *Econ. Innov. New Techn.*, 17(7-8):717-729.

② See: Siegel, D., Wright, M., Chapple, W. and Lockett, A., 2008. Assessing the relative performance of university technology transfer in the US and UK: A stochastic distance function approach. *Econ. Innov. New Techn.*, 17(7-8):717-729.

③ See: Siegel, D., Wright, M., Chapple, W. and Lockett, A., 2008. Assessing the relative performance of university technology transfer in the US and UK: A stochastic distance function approach. *Econ. Innov. New Techn.*, 17(7-8):717-729.

④Caulfield, T., 2012. Should scientists have to always show the commercial benefits of their research? Available at https://policyoptions. irpp. org/magazines/talking - science/caulfield/, accessed 23 September 2020.

ies would never make it to the clinic.[①] Diminishing this risk requires TTO's staff to find relevant access to valuable, appropriate and cost-effective processes for each technology transfer. Poyago-Theotoky, J., Beath, J. and Siegel, D.S. (2002) find that funding initiatives aimed at promoting technology partnerships also stimulated university-industry collaborations[②], which is also one of the dimensions for overcoming this risk.

According to Link, A.N. and Siegel, D.S. (2005), university administrators who wish to foster the university-industry technology transfer process should be mindful of the importance of financial incentives.[③] Budget and financial resources for TTO are very important issues. Universities are experiencing increased pressure to generate revenue from licensing and innovation activities. But university leaders must recognize that successful economic engagement will not be focused on short-term income but rather on longer-term work on relationship development and ecosystem building. Some universities develop early-stage proof-of-concept funds[④] as well as government funding. Pace survey suggests that government funding provides an important means for expanding technological opportunities open to firms.[⑤] According to the European Commission (EU), it currently has a target of investing 3% of GDP in research and development, and the aim is by connecting research and development and innovation to get a broader range of expenditure which would be more rele-

① Ibid.

② Poyago-Theotoky, J., Beath, J. and Siegel, D.S., 2002. Universities and fundamental research: reflections on the growth of university-industry partnerships. *Oxford Review of Economic Policy*, 18(1):6.

③ See: Link, A.N. and Siegel, D.S., 2005. Generating science-based growth: an econometric analysis of the impact of organizational incentives on university-industry technology transfer. *European Journal of Finance*, 11(3):169–181.

④ See: Michigan State University Innovation Center, Advance Grant Proof-of-Concept Fund available at https://innovationcenter.msu.edu/advance, accessed 23 September 2020.

⑤ Salter, A.J. and Martin, B.R., 2001. The economic benefits of publicly funded basic research: a critical review. *Research policy*, 30(3):521.

潜在有益的基础科学发现将永远无法进入正轨[①]。减少这种风险需要技术转移办公室工作人员针对技术转移的每一种情况，都能找到适当且具有成本效益的实用程序。此外，在促进技术伙伴关系的筹资举措也促进了大学与产业的合作，这也是克服财务风险的一种方式[②]。

希望促进大学与行业技术转移进程的管理者[③]应注重财政激励的重要性。技术转移办公室的预算和财政资源也是非常重要的问题。大学面临着从许可证和创新活动中获得收入的压力。但是，成功的经济参与不会侧重于短期收入，而是侧重于关系发展和生态系统建设的长期工作。一些高校开发了早期阶段的概念验证基金及政府资助[④]，调查表明，政府资助为扩大向企业开放的技术机会提供了重要手段[⑤]。根据欧盟委员会（EU）的说法，欧盟目前的目标是将国内生产总值的3%投资于研究和开发，其目的是将研究和开发与创新联系起来，以获得更广泛的产出，这将更适合商业

①Ibid.

② Poyago-Theotoky, J., Beath, J. and Siegel, D.S., 2002. Universities and fundamental research: reflections on the growth of university - industry partnerships. *Oxford Review of Economic Policy*, 18(1):6.

③ See: Link, A.N. and Siegel, D.S., 2005. Generating science-based growth: an econometric analysis of the impact of organizational incentives on university - industry technology transfer. *European Journal of Finance*, 11(3):169–181.

④ See: Michigan State University Innovation Center, Advance Grant Proof-of-Concept Fund available at https://innovationcenter.msu.edu/advance, accessed 23 September 2020.

⑤ Salter, A.J. and Martin, B.R., 2001. The economic benefits of publicly funded basic research: a critical review. *Research policy*, 30(3):521.

vant for business operations and for productivity drivers.①

3.2.2 Risks related to the businesses

The prevailing conviction throughout the private sector is that engaging in technology transfer process can be risky and too expensive. But, as Frey argues, all companies deal with risk; there is a risk in doing something, and there is risk in doing nothing.② Risk is a part of being in business, and how the organization is prepared to manage risk is a leading factor in its ability to move into new competitive arenas.③ Diminishing this risk needs TTOs to develop powerful and user-friendly proofs about the real impact of TTOs on the private sector.④ Today, firms are reluctant to take on the risk of commercializing unproven inventions.⑤ Therefore, TTOs need to be more aggressive toward universities/research organizations in regard to their investment in money and efforts for prototypes and other appropriate proofs for invention's effectiveness. Additionally, TTOs should be more aggressive toward universities regarding their investment in disclosing all inventions to the TTO and should build research capacity accordingly to provide the private sector opportunities. TTOs must assess a market's readiness for the invention as well.

The private sector's failure to recognize, absorb and turn into commercial-success inventions is the next risk. Diminishing this risk requires TTOs to take more aggressive initiatives toward policymakers to improve the overall performance of technology transfer process. Besides, TTO should develop programs which bring together businesses, industry, universities, and government in ways to understand that they

---

① European Commission (EC), 2010. Europe 2020: A strategy for smart, sustainable and inclusive growth. *Working paper {COM* (2010) 2020}: 8

② Frey, Chuck. 2009. "What is an Innovation Culture?" Innovation Management, available at http://www.innovationmanagement.se/imtool-articles/what-is-an-innovation-culture/, accessed 23 September 2020.

③ Ibid.

④ See: "AUTM Better World Project" available at https://autm.net/about-tech-transfer/better-world-project, accessed 23 September 2020.

⑤ House of Commons Canada. 2017. "Intellectual Property and Technology Transfer: Promoting Best Practices Report of the Standing Committee on Industry, Science and Technology.": 18.

运作和生产力的推动[1]。

3.2.2 与企业相关的风险

所有私营企业普遍认为，参与技术转移过程可能面临高风险高成本。但是，所有公司都面临风险，做任何事都存在风险，什么事不做也是有风险的[2]。风险是业务中的一部分，组织如何准备管理风险是公司进入新竞争领域能力的一个主导因素[3]。减少这种风险需要技术转移办公室就其对私营企业的实际影响制定有力和用户友好的证据[4]。如今，企业不愿承担将未经证实的发明商业化的风险[5]。因此技术转移办公室需要积极提升大学或研究机构在资金投资和对原型以及发明有效性投资的回报率。此外，技术转移办公室应更积极地向大学投资，大学向技术转移办公室披露所有发明，并相应地巩固研究能力，为私营部门提供机会。技术转移办公室还必须评估该发明的市场准备情况。

另一个风险是，私营部门未能承认、吸收这些发明，并将其转化为成功商业化的发明。减少这种风险需要技术和技术服务部门对私营企业采取更积极主动的行动，以改善技术转移过程的总体表现。此外，技术转移办公室应该开发将企业、工业、大学和政府结合在一起的项目，以

---

① European Commission (EC), 2010. Europe 2020: A strategy for smart, sustainable and inclusive growth. *Working paper* {*COM* (2010) 2020}:8

② Frey, Chuck. 2009. "What is an Innovation Culture?" Innovation Management, available at http.//www.innovationmanagcmcnt.sc/imtool articlcs/what is an innovation culturc/, acccssed 23 September 2020.

③ Ibid.

④ See: "AUTM Better World Project" available at https://autm.net/about-tech-transfer/better-world-project, accessed 23 September 2020.

⑤ House of Commons Canada. 2017. "Intellectual Property and Technology Transfer: Promoting Best Practices Report of the Standing Committee on Industry, Science and Technology.": 18.

have common objectives.

3.2.3 Risks related to the universities/research organizations

The initial risk in this group is connected to the invention disclosure. Jensen, R. A., Thursby, J.G. and Thursby, M.C (2003) find that the TTOs reported licensing objectives are influenced by their views of faculty and administration, which supports the assumption that the TTO is a dual agent.① One of the main risks is that academics do not share their findings with TTOs because of different reasons: lack of awareness of the researcher about the potential commercialization value of their research, or academics might bring the best ideas into commercial application outside the university, without reporting to the TTO.② According to Leyden, D.P. and Link, A.N. (2015), the inventor's decision to disclose is influenced by the university's reward systems and culture. If the university has a reward system in place that provides incentives for faculty to engage in commercialization activities, the inventor might be more likely to disclose and participate in the formal mechanisms of technology transfer.③ If there are too many perceived barriers and disadvantages to involving the TTO and going through official channels, the inventor might circumvent disclosure and adopt informal mechanisms of technology transfer.④ University faculty and students are also motivated by the potential income they may derive from the commercialization of their inventions, as well as the satisfaction from seeing their inventions put to good use (often for the public good).⑤ These questions should be part of the TTO's initiative toward policymakers to improve the technology transfer process's overall

① See: Jensen, R.A., Thursby, J.G. and Thursby, M.C., 2003. Disclosure and licensing of University inventions: 'The best we can do with the s**t we get to work with'. *International Journal of Industrial Organization*, 21(9):1271–1300.

② Ibid.

③ Leyden, D.P. and Link, A.N., 2015. *Public sector entrepreneurship: US technology and innovation policy.* Oxford University Press, USA:104.

④ Ibid.

⑤ University of Pretoria Contract and Innovation Office, Innovation and Technology Transfer, available at https://www.up.ac.za/contracts-innovation-office/article/262155/innovation-technology-transfer, accessed 23 September 2020.

理解他们的共同目标。

3.2.3　与大学研究组织有关的风险

技术转移办公室报告最初的风险受到他们对员工和管理看法的影响，这证明了技术转移办公室是双重代理的假设①。这其中的主要风险之一是，由于对其研究的潜在商业化价值缺乏认识，或者可能会将最佳想法带到大学以外的商业应用中而不向技术转移办公室报告②，研究人员无法向技术转移办公室分享他们的研究结果。而研究人员是否披露发明的决定受到大学奖励制度和文化的影响。如果大学有奖励制度，能为从事商业化活动提供奖励，研究人员更加有可能披露和参与技术转移③。如果技术转移办公室和官方渠道存在太多的障碍和缺点，研究人员可能会规避披露，并采用非正式的技术转移机制④。大学教职员工和学生会因他们的发明商业化而带来的潜在收入获得激励，发明也会得到很好的利用（通常是为了公共利益）而感到满意⑤。为了提高技术转移进程的总体绩效，这些问题应成为技术转移办公室决策者倡议的一部分。

---

① See: Jensen, R.A., Thursby, J.G. and Thursby, M.C., 2003. Disclosure and licensing of University inventions: 'The best we can do with the s**t we get to work with'. *International Journal of Industrial Organization*, 21(9):1271–1300.

② Ibid.

③ Leyden, D.P. and Link, A.N., 2015. *Public sector entrepreneurship: US technology and innovation policy*. Oxford University Press, USA:104.

④ Ibid.

⑤ University of Pretoria Contract and Innovation Office, Innovation and Technology Transfer, available at https://www.up.ac.za/contracts-innovation-office/article/262155/innovation-technology-transfer, accessed 23 September 2020.

performance.

The role of scientists employed at universities is the next risk. Scientists employed in many universities play the roles of teachers and lecturers and have no enough time for research. Diminishing this risk needs changes in the universities' working model. These solutions should not take any form of pressure on the researchers and faculty staff to focus on rapid research commercialization.

3.2.4 State policy

Bureaucracy and complexity of regulations, unfriendly procedures, tax systems require a lot of time and money, and this does not encourage research organizations and businesses to collaborate jointly. These questions should be part of the TTO's initiative toward policymakers in order to improve the overall performance of technology transfer system.

Policies on IP and costs connected to IP protection are very tough questions for all participants in technology transfer process. Consequently, they must be coherent, transparent, clearly defined and applied consistently.

3.2.5 Innovation culture

Innovation culture seen as willingness for taking risks; openness to discovery and experimentation; readiness for new skills, should be created. TTOs should work on building an atmosphere that inspires the society to seek out innovative opportunities through courses and educational experiences, improvement of curriculum to better educate and develop entrepreneurs, training and courses related to innovation, places students with campus researchers to identify commercialization pathways, nationally-recognized programs for cooperative education, internships and experiential learning programs inherently build links with industry partners, government agencies and not-for-profit organizations.[①] In this regard, the foundation of a special technology transfer course is a great way to develop a strong foundation for people linked directly or indirectly to technology transfer process. At the same time, it develops the opportunities to learn from a network, with benefits for TTOs and society.

---

① See: Memorial University, Technology Transfer and Commercialization Office, 2015. Technology Transfer and Commercialization Strategy.

在大学工作的科研人员的角色则是另一个风险。他们承担日常教学任务，没有足够的时间进行研究。减少这种风险则需要改变大学工作模式，使研究人员和教职员工专注于推动发明研究商业化。

3.2.4 国家政策

官僚主义和复杂的法规、不友好的程序、税收制度、大量的时间和金钱成本，都不利于研究人员和企业合作。为了提高技术转移系统的整体性能，这些问题应该是技术转移办公室决策者做出决策时应当考虑规避的。

同时，知识产权的政策和与知识产权保护有关的费用对技术转移过程的所有参与者来说都是非常棘手的问题，因此，知识产权的政策和与知识产权保护有关的费用必须公开透明、始终如一，并且可以延续执行。

3.2.5 创新文化

创新文化也就是愿意承担风险，对发现和实验持开放态度，对接受新技能有所准备。技术转移办公室应努力营造氛围，鼓励社会通过教育来寻求创新机会：改进课程和丰富教育经历提升学力以教育和培养企业家，开设与创新相关的培训和课程，安排学生与高校研究人员一起确定商业化途径。国家认可的合作教育、实习和体验式学习项目与行业合作伙伴、政府机构和非营利组织有着内在的联系[①]。在此基础上，开设特定的技术转移课程，为帮助与技术转移过程中的直接/间接联系人打下坚实的基础。同时，开发通过网络学习的机会，这对技术转移办公室和社会都有好处。

① See: Memorial University, Technology Transfer and Commercialization Office, 2015. Technology Transfer and Commercialization Strategy.

Knowing and "safely" handling risks associated with the TTOs required a deep understanding of the technology transfer process. This understanding helps guide decisions and risk management while navigating the process of technology commercialization.[①]

① See: Bashir, S., 2014. Risk in University Technology Transfer. *King Abdullah University of Science and technology, Innovation and Economic Development*, available at https://innovation.kaust.edu.sa/risk-university-technology-transfer/.

了解和“安全”处理与技术转移办公室相关的风险需要技术转移部门理解技术转移过程，这种理解有助于在技术商业化进程中指导决策，进行风险管理[1]。

① See: Bashir, S., 2014. Risk in University Technology Transfer. *King Abdullah University of Science and technology, Innovation and Economic Development*, available at https://innovation.kaust.edu.sa/risk-university-technology-transfer/.

4 ESTABLISHING TECHNOLOGY TRANSFER OFFICE

4.1 Essential conditions required for the creation of an effective TTO

Essential conditions necessary for building an effective TTO are quite similar to the essential conditions required for the creation of an effective technology transfer system. These conditions could be summarized in these major factors: national economic strategy, national intellectual property (IP) system, human resources, capital and scientific research. These factors are interlinked as described below.

4.1.1 National economic strategy

In today's world, one of the most significant and crucial leaders of development is information and knowledge. The principal goal of technology transfer for society and the national economy is to create a partnership between academia and the private sector,[①] and TTOs are centers which play an important role within research and assessment of research results toward the application of technologies in the private sector.[②] Even the knowledge is widely accepted by companies as a very important

① See: Swiss Technology Transfer available at https://switt.ch/swiss-technology-transfer.
② Ibid.

第四章　建立技术转移办公室

4.1　创建技术转移办公室的基本条件

建立有效的技术转移办公室的基本条件与建立有效的技术转移系统的基本条件非常相似。这些条件可以概括为以下5种因素：国家经济战略、国家知识产权（IP）制度、人力资源、资本和科学研究，这些因素相互关联。

4.1.1　国家经济战略

当今世界发展的最重要的要素是信息和知识。对社会和国民经济来说，技术转移的主要目的是在学术界和私营企业之间建立伙伴关系[①]，技术转移办公室是研究和评估私营企业技术应用研究成果的中心[②]。即使知识被公司广泛接受为非常重要的组成部分，知识开发潜力也没有得到很好

① See: Swiss Technology Transfer available at https://switt.ch/swiss-technology-transfer.

② Ibid.

component, the knowledge development potential is not well exploited.① Among other reasons which could change this situation is to start making technology transfer a part of the national economic strategy, but then developing a separate national strategy for technology transfer. The national economic strategy should be encouraging and supportive in relation to TTOs and aimed at removing barriers that limit the success of TTOs. The base of this strategy should be best practices and policies in the area of technology transfer, related national and international reports and studies as well as broad discussions and decisions made jointly with stakeholders. The adequate and applicable solutions in this field are directly linked with the legislators' consistent policies and awareness (IP rights, taxation, education and research). Lawmakers and governments should play the role of a helpful guide for the researches, research, IP protection and university-business connections. Technology transfer should be an inevitable part of the national economic and innovation strategy, especially development support programs of technology transfer, technology transfer ecosystems, and technology transfer critical infrastructure. Governments should make research and innovation policies more responsive to contemporary trends. Also, adaptation and evaluation of the implementation of the policies in support of technology transfer and commercialization ought to be done in a continuum. This is the technique for a national strategy to have a direct positive impact on the creation and effectiveness of TTOs.

4.1.2 National Intellectual Property (IP) system

Intellectual property (IP) is the overall term for property in the creation of the mind, including inventions, literary and artistic works, but also designs, names and images used in commerce.② Intellectual property rights (IP) are private legal rights that protect the previously described creation of the human mind. There are two dis-

① Neumann, G. and Tomé, E., 2011. The Changing Role of Knowledge in Companies: How to Improve Business Performance Through Knowledge. *Electronic Journal of Knowledge Management*, 9(1).

② World Health Organization, 2020. Intellectual Property, available at https://www.who.int/topics/intellectual_property/en/, accessed 20 September 2020.

的开发①。改变这种情况的原因之一是，政府开始将技术转移作为国民经济战略的一部分，进而制定单独的国家技术转移战略，国家经济战略应鼓励和支持技术贸易机会，旨在消除限制技术转移的障碍。这一战略的基础应是技术转移领域的最佳做法，是政策相关的国家和国际报告和研究，以及与利益相关者共同进行的广泛讨论后做出的决定。在这一领域，适当和适用的解决办法与立法者的政策和意识（知识产权、税收、教育和研究的一致性）直接相关。立法者和政府应该为研究、知识产权保护和大学—企业联系发挥有益的指导作用。技术转移应是国民经济和创新战略的必然组成部分，特别是技术转移发展支持计划、技术转移生态系统和技术转移关键基础设施。各国政府应使研究和创新政策更适应当代趋势。此外，应连续不断地调整和评价支持技术转移和商业化政策的执行情况。这是国家战略对技术贸易机会的建立和有效性产生直接积极影响的因素。

4.1.2　国家知识产权（IP）制度

知识产权（IP）是智力创造成果的总称，包括发明、文学和艺术作品，也包括商业中使用的设计、名称和图像。② 知识产权（IP）是保护先前描述的人类思维创造的私人法律权利。知识产权有两种不同的类别：一是版权，包括文学艺术作品和工业财产；二是产权，包括专利、商标、工

①Neumann, G. and Tomé, E., 2011. The Changing Role of Knowledge in Companies: How to Improve Business Performance Through Knowledge. *Electronic Journal of Knowledge Management*, 9(1).

②World Health Organization, 2020. Intellectual Property, available at https://www.who.int/topics/intellectual_property/en/, accessed 20 September 2020.

tinct categories of IP: copyright, which includes literary and artistic works and industrial property, which includes inventions protected by patents, trademarks, industrial designs, and geographical indications.①

IP is protected by law. This protection actually secures recognition and benefits for the IP holders. European Commission highlights that protection and enforcement of intellectual property are crucial for the state's ability to stimulate innovation and compete globally.② IP infrastructure, updated IP laws and regulations are essential for TTOs. IP laws are relevant not only to owners of IP but also to funders, innovators, competitors, consumers and governments – in fact, these laws can be viewed as a bargain between the rightsholder and the state.③ Also, an essential characteristic of the legislative framework regarding IP is its clarity. The national legal framework about IP should regulate IP ownership, especially researchers' rights on inventions, IP ownership of publicly funded research. The goal of IP laws should be to promote, protect and facilitate the place and role of innovation in a competitive marketplace. IP laws and policymakers should aspire to maintain a balance between protecting innovators against anti-competitive practices and foster a public for the benefit of future innovators.④

One of the most important debates regarding technology transfer and TTOs is about the best IP ownership model for academic institutions. Different countries have different ways of legislating on this matter. Ownership rights within a university typically fall into three categories: inventor-owned, institution-owned or jointly-owned.⑤

---

① Ibid.

② European Commission, 2019. Intellectual Property, available at http://ec.europa.eu/trade/policy/accessing-markets/intellectual-property/, accessed 20 September 2020.

③ Royal Society (Great Britain), 2003. *Keeping Science Open: The Effects of Intellectual Property on the Conduct of Science*. Royal Society: 1.

④ House of Commos Chamber Des Communes Canada, 2017. Intellectual Property and Technology Transfer: Promoting Best Practices, Report of the Standing Committee on Industry, Science and Technology: 15.

⑤ Memorial University, Technology Transfer and Commercialization Office, 2015. Technology Transfer and Commercialization Strategy: 10.

业设计和地理标志保护的发明[①]。

知识产权受法律保护。这种保护实际上确保了知识产权持有人的权利。欧盟委员会强调，保护和执行知识产权对于国家刺激创新和在全球经济中的竞争力至关重要[②]。知识产权基础设施、更新的知识产权法律和法规对技术转移办公室也至关重要。知识产权法不仅与知识产权的所有者有关，而且与资助者、创新者、竞争对手、消费者和政府都有关。事实上，这些法律可以被视为所有者和国家之间的讨价还价[③]。此外，关于知识产权的立法框架的一个非常重要的特点是明确性。关于知识产权的国家法律框架应规范知识产权所有权，特别是研究人员的发明权、公共资助研究的知识产权所有权。知识产权法的目标应该是促进和保护创新在市场竞争中的地位和作用。知识产权法和决策者应力求在保护创新者免受反竞争做法之害和培养共同体以造福未来创新者之间保持平衡[④]。

关于技术转移和技术转移办公室的主要争论之一是学术机构知识产权所有权的最佳模式。不同的国家有不同的立法方式，但大学内的所有权通常分为三类：发明家拥有、机构拥有或共同拥有[⑤]。对文献、研究和实践

① Ibid.

② European Commission, 2019. Intellectual Property, available at http://ec.europa.eu/trade/policy/accessing-markets/intellectual-property/, accessed 20 September 2020.

③ Royal Society (Great Britain), 2003. *Keeping Science Open: The Effects of Intellectual Property on the Conduct of Science*. Royal Society: 1.

④House of Commos Chamber Des Communes Canada, 2017. Intellectual Property and Technology Transfer: Promoting Best Practices, Report of the Standing Committee on Industry, Science and Technology: 15.

⑤Memorial University, Technology Transfer and Commercialization Office, 2015. Technology Transfer and Commercialization Strategy: 10.

Reviews of the literature, research studies and practice show that each model has positive and negative attributes, but also either approach can work well.[①] Accordingly, there is no most successful IP model expected to have the most successful outcomes for each university and each TTO. The result is many different ownership models, i.e., different universities with different policies. Different universities with different policies are not easy tasks for TTO because it asks having a lot of information, knowledge and negotiations as pre - activities which is usually a difficult process. But, having in mind the varieties in industries and business, this solution for different university IP policies could be effective. Much more important for the industry as well as for the universities is to execute their own policies effectively, transparently and consistently. In our opinion, effective IP policies in favor of the technology transfer process could be developed only jointly by stakeholders, lawmakers and policymakers.

At the same time, there is no doubt that the success of the technology transfer, commercialization and TTOs depend on the faculty members' perception of the technology transfer process and their engagement in the whole process. Accordingly, faculty members should be motivated to do so.

Countries should develop national IP and innovation strategies governing IP ownership, but another very important step in the development of TTOs is the development of specific technology transfer regulations.

The development of IP system should be guided by the aim to foster an environment in which creativity and innovation can flourish.[②] It brings us back to the main characteristics of the IP policies and legislation: flexible, clear and transparent,

① See: Young, A.T., 2007. Establishing a Technology Transfer Office, In Intellectual Property Management in Health and Agricultural Innovation: A Handbook of Best Practices (eds. A Krattiger, RT Mahoney, L Nelsen, et al.). MIHR: Oxford, U.K., and PIPRA: Davis, U.S.A; Memorial University, Technology Transfer and Commercialization Office, 2015. Technology Transfer and Commercialization Strategy: 20.

② See: University of Plymouth, what is IP?, available at: https://www.plymouth.ac.uk/research/support/intellectual-property/intellectual-property-faqs/what-is-ip, accessed 20 September 2020.

的回顾表明，每个模式都有积极和消极的属性，但任何一种方法都能很好地起作用①。因此，没有一个绝对成功的知识产权模型完全保证为每所大学和每一项技术转移办公室取得最成功的结果。其结果是产生了许多不同的所有权模式，即：不同的大学有不同的政策，这是一项艰巨的任务，因为它要求有大量的信息、知识和谈判作为前期活动，这通常是一个复杂的过程。但是考虑到产业和商业的多样性，这种针对不同大学知识产权政策的解决方案可能是有效的。对产业和大学来说，更重要的是一致的、透明的、清晰的和延续执行的政策。我们认为，利益攸关方、法律制定者和决策者应当共同制定有利于技术转移进程的有效知识产权政策。

同时，毫无疑问，技术转移、商业化和技术转移的成功取决于教职员工对技术转移过程的看法及其在整个过程中的参与。

各国应制定国家知识产权和管理知识产权所有权的创新战略，而技术转移办公室发展的另一个非常重要的工作是制定具体的技术转移条例。

知识产权制度的发展应以促进创造和创新蓬勃发展的环境为目标②。回到知识产权政策和立法的主要特点，即：灵活、清晰和透明来看，就是让大学能够根据自己的具体需要选择自己的政策。

①See: Young, A.T., 2007. Establishing a Technology Transfer Office, In Intellectual Property Management in Health and Agricultural Innovation: A Handbook of Best Practices (eds. A Krattiger, RT Mahoney, L Nelsen, et al.). MIHR: Oxford, U.K., and PIPRA: Davis, U.S.A; Memorial University, Technology Transfer and Commercialization Office, 2015. Technology Transfer and Commercialization Strategy:20.

② See: University of Plymouth, What is IP?, available at: https://www.plymouth.ac.uk/research/support/intellectual-property/intellectual-property-faqs/what-is-ip, accessed 20 September 2020.

which allows the universities to choose their policies according to their specific needs.

A particularly significant part of the effective IP system is a well-developed national IP infrastructure, which will facilitate cooperation with the TTOs and deliver more efficient services. This means, besides flexible, clear and transparent law and policies, essentials for well-developed TTOs and technology transfer are also: technical infrastructure, standards, databases, new technologies, digital services of different kinds as well as a variety of tools.

4.1.3 Human recourses

Keeping in mind TTO's activities and tasks, staffing a TTO is a big challenge. The major question is, what are the most important/needed skills and abilities of TTO staff? In line with the TTO's activities, it is evident that TTO staff should possess scientific, legal, communication and business skills and expertise. Personnel requirements will depend on the institution, the volume of work and the mandate of the TTO:[①] TTO may be arranged as an interdisciplinary team of people, or a single individual that is capable of leveraging the necessary support from external experts[②]. Also, in the case of TTO, a very significant question for the whole technology transfer process is timely fulfillment of the administrative duties, daily telephone and e-mail correspondence, maintaining websites, handling documents. This ongoing work must be efficient. Therefore, TTOs need administrative staff too.

When talking about human resources and TTO, it is worthy of noting that cooperation, support and contact between relevant stakeholders are also essential (See Figure 3).

---

① Organization mondiale de la propriété intellectuelle, 2007. *Technology transfer, intellectual property and effective university-industry partnerships: the experience of China, India, Japan, Philippines, the Republic of Korea, Singapore and Thailand*: 44.

② Ibid.

有效的知识产权制度的重要作用之一是发展良好的国家知识产权基础设施，这将促进与技术转移办公室的合作并提供更有效的服务。这意味着，除了灵活、明确和透明的法律和政策外，发展良好的技术转移办公室和技术转移的基本要素还包括技术基础设施、标准、数据库、新技术、各种数字服务以及各种工具。

4.1.3　人力资源

考虑到技术转移办公室的活动和任务，配置技术转移办公室是一个巨大的挑战，主要问题是技术转移办公室员工最重要且最需要的技能和能力是什么？根据技术转移办公室的工作，技术转移办公室工作人员显然应具备科学、法律、沟通和业务的技能和专门知识，人员需求将取决于机构、工作量和技术转移办公室的任务[①]。技术转移办公室可以安排有跨学科的人员团队，或者一个能够利用外部专家的必要支持的个人[②]。此外，在整个技术转移过程中要及时履行行政职责，接听电话、回复邮件、维护网站、处理文档，这些工作必须做到有效执行。因此，技术转移办公室也需要行政人员。

在讨论人力资源和技术转移办公室时，值得注意的是，相关利益攸关方之间的合作、支持和联系也是必不可少的（见图3）。

① Organisation mondiale de la propriété intellectuelle, 2007. *Technology transfer, intellectual property and effective university-industry partnerships: the experience of China, India, Japan, Philippines, the Republic of Korea, Singapore and Thailand*:44.

② Ibid.

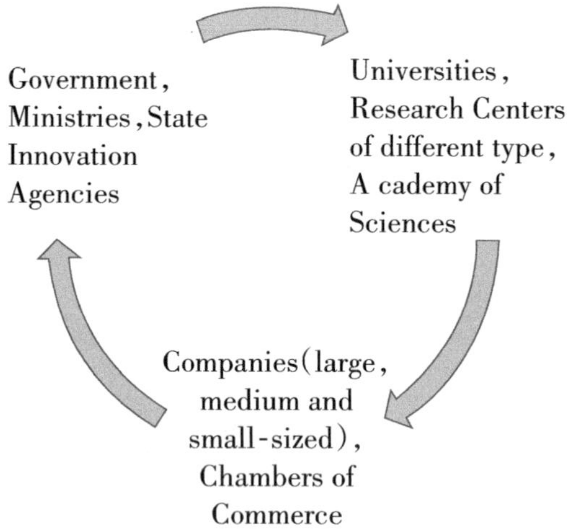

Figure 3 Main stakeholders of the technology transfer

In this regard, legislators and public administration have an important role. They have a position that enables them to be close to both parties' science and practice. Therefore, they should first establish and support the environment suitable for the cooperation of all participants. They have the power to arrange a lot of activities, essential for the university - industry technology transfer process. Therefore, they should provide meetings with all the participants, they can identify currently support options, facilitate the involvement of other potential partners and experts, organize other supporting services (e.g. project management), they can mediate potential conflicts, and help to overcome barriers such as a state of "not-know", "not-do" or "not-want", and thereby they promote scientific and technological transfer.①

4.1.4 Capital

Taking into account, TTO's activities, pre - activities and tasks, as well as TTO staffing, it is obvious that efficient TTO needs capital. This capital comes from public and private funds. The universal view is that university - industry transfer requires considerable resources. One expert interviewed for the study Understanding

① Apax Partners is an independent global partnership focused solely on long-term investment in growth companies. Funds advised by Apax Partners typically invest in large companies with an enterprise value between €1bn and €5bn. See at: https://www.apax.com/inside-apax/company/, accessed 21 September 2020.

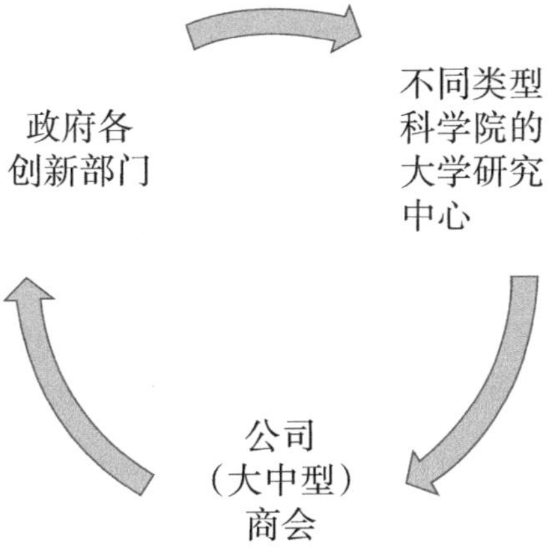

图3　技术转移的主要利益攸关方

在这方面，立法者和公共行政部门发挥着重要作用。立法者和公共行政部门的立场使他们能够接近双方的科学和实践。因此，他们应首先建立和支持适合所有参与者合作的环境，可行使其权力安排大量的活动，这对大学—行业的技术转移过程至关重要。所以，立法者或公共行政部门应与所有与会者进行会议，确定目前的资助方案，促进其他潜在伙伴和专家的参与，组织其他支撑性服务（例如：项目管理），也可以调解潜在的冲突，帮助克服诸如“不知道”“不做”或“不想”等障碍，从而促进科学和技术转移[①]。

4.1.4　资本

就技术转移办公室的前期筹建、运营、任务执行以及人员配置等因素而言，很明显，一个高效的技术转移办公室需要资金支持。资金可能来自公共资金或私人资金。人们普遍认为，大学—产业转移需要相当多的资金支持。

① Apax Partners is an independent global partnership focused solely on long-term investment in growth companies. Funds advised by Apax Partners typically invest in large companies with an enterprise value between €1bn and €5bn. See at: https://www.apax.com/inside-apax/company/, accessed 21 September 2020.

Technology Transfer[①] estimated that US$1,000 worth of academic intellectual property needed between US$1m and US$10m of development effort to turn it into a usable product.[②] When talking about capital needed for TTOs, we have to keep in mind that this cost is not connected only directly with TTOs, but also with other factors. Thus, the capital needed for TTOs should also be analyzed through the IP protection costs, availability and complexity of IP protection, research budget, years needed for the development of scientific research to market product and availability of commercialization funds and complexity of procedures. The comprehensive observation of this question showed that low activity in terms of patent registration and commercialization is also the result of complex and expensive IP protection.[③]

Access to finances that support innovation and university-technology may also depend on sectors. Among the existing financial instruments are innovation vouchers, business angels, venture capital, bankable projects, accelerators and incubators, grants and university seed funds.

All the TTO opportunities are connected to the research. Clearly, the research budget is also among the required essentials. The economy that invests most in research and development is the United States, followed by China and the European Union. The U.S. government invests some $135B each year to advance science and technology as the basis for breakthrough knowledge development and innovations. Of which around 20 to 30 percent is invested in successful technology transfer.[④] Gross

① Available at: https://www.wipo.int/export/sites/www/sme/en/newsletter/2011/attachments/apax_tech_transfer.pdf, accessed 21 September 2020.

② See: Apax, Understanding technology transfer, available at https://www.unemed.com/wp-content/uploads/2015/06/apax_tech_transfer.pdf, accessed 21 September 2020.

③ Apax Partners is an independent global partnership focused solely on long-term investment in growth companies. Funds advised by Apax Partners typically invest in large companies with an enterprise value between €1bn and €5bn. See at: https://www.apax.com/inside-apax/company/, accessed 21 September 2020.

④ Barbur, 2018. Unlocking the Potential for Successful Technology Transfer, available at https://www.rdworldonline.com/unlocking-the-potential-for-successful-technology-transfer/, accessed 21 September 2020.

据一位接受《技术转移的理解》[①]这一调研采访的专家估计，价值1000美元的学术知识产权需要100万美元到1000万美元的投入才能将其变成可用的产品[②]。当谈论技术转移办公室所需的资金时，我们必须记住，这种成本不仅与技术转移办公室直接相关，而且与其他因素也有关系。因此，还应通过知识产权保护成本、知识产权保护的可用性和复杂性、研究预算、将科学研究发展到市场产品所需的年份以及商业化资金的可用性和程序的复杂性来分析技术贸易机会所需的资金。对这一问题的广泛研究表明，在专利注册和商业化方面的低活跃度也是复杂和昂贵的知识产权保护的结果[③]。

获得支持创新和大学技术的资金也可能取决于各个部门。现有的金融工具包括创新券、商业天使、风险投资、可担保项目、加速器和孵化器、捐款、大学种子基金等。

所有的技术转移办公室几乎都与研究有关。显然，研究预算也是必要的要素之一。目前，世界上投资最多的国家是美国，其次是中国和欧盟成员国。美国政府每年投资约1350亿美元，作为突破性的知识开发和新创新的基础，用于推动科学技术的发展。其中约20%至30%投资于成功的技术转移[④]。欧盟各成员国研究和发展的国内支出总额在2017年为每年3170

① Available at：https://www.wipo.int/export/sites/www/sme/en/newsletter/2011/attachments/apax_tech_transfer.pdf，accessed 21 September 2020.

② See：Apax，Understanding technology transfer，available at https://www.unemed.com/wp-content/uploads/2015/06/apax_tech_transfer.pdf，accessed 21 September 2020.

③ Apax Partners is an independent global partnership focused solely on long-term investment in growth companies. Funds advised by Apax Partners typically invest in large companies with an enterprise value between €1bn and €5bn. See at：https://www.apax.com/inside-apax/company/，accessed 21 September 2020.

④ Barbur，2018. Unlocking the Potential for Successful Technology Transfer，available at https://www.rdworldonline.com/unlocking-the-potential-for-successful-technology-transfer/，accessed 21 September 2020.

domestic expenditure on research and development in the European Union was EUR 317 billion a year in 2017, equal to 2.06% of GDP.[①] But, China is becoming a leader of innovating in the world. This dominance is measured through data for investment in the research and development, international patents, increased highly-cited scientific research, as well as grooving importance of China in the development of new technologies and digitalization.[②]

From the industry's point of view, the features of effective technology transfer and effective TTO are the following: academic research proper to business, curriculum prepared industry and business's needs accordingly. These demands are connected to financial support. From this perspective, university-industry/businesses financial support can be developed through mutual granting too: participation of faculty and students in the industry; participation of industry scientists in the academy; development of mutual research projects; development of future opportunities employment of students.

Many countries' private sectors lack the financial capacity to absorb academic IP and turn it into commercial success. This situation must be taken into account by policymakers in order to improve the use of TTOs. In view of this, public funding through key programmers supporting technology transfer and TTO's activities should be provided. These key programmers should mitigate the risk of TTO activities. For example,[③] commercialization coupons in order to fund technology transfer activities; require that universities direct a percentage of all public funds granted to support research to technology transfer activities; fund twice what universities earn in IP revenues; funding programs designed for directly benefit for SMEs participating in technology transfer; creating a funding program that matches a certain amount of govern-

① European Investment Bank, 2019. *Investment Report 2019/2020 Accelerating Europe's Transformation*. Economics Department (EIB): 113.

② Ibid.

③ See: House of Commons–Canada, Standing Committee on Industry, Science and Technology, 2017. *Intellectual Property and Technology Transfer: Promoting Best Practices Report*, available at https://www.ourcommons.ca/Content/Committee/421/INDU/Reports/RP9261888/indurp08/indurp08-e.pdf, accessed 21 September 2020.

亿欧元，相当于其国内生产总值的2.06%[①]。但是，中国正在成为世界创新的领导者。这种优势是通过对研究和开发的投资、国际专利、高级科学研究的增加以及中国在发展新技术和数字化方面的重要性的数据来衡量的[②]。

从行业的角度来看，有效的技术转移和技术转移办公室的特点是具有适合商业的学术研究和适合相应的行业和企业需求的课程，这些需求与财政支持有关。从这个角度来看，大学—企业的财政支持也可以通过相互给予来发展，教师和学生参与企业，企业科学家参与学术，发展相互研究项目，为学生未来就业创造机会。

许多国家的私营企业缺乏吸收学术知识产权并将其成功转化为商业的财政能力。决策者必须考虑到这种情况，以便更好地利用技术转移机会。鉴于此，应通过支持技术转移和技术转移办公室的活动制定关键方案，这些关键方案应减少技术贸易机会活动的风险，主要包括[③]为技术转移活动提供资金的商业化优惠券；要求各大学提供一定比例的公共资金，用于支持技术转移活动的研究；提供两倍于大学知识产权收入的资金；为参与技术转移的中小企业直接受益而设计的工资方案；制订一份工资方案，将一定数量的政府资金与私营企业提供的资金相匹配；发展学生孵化器；在协作环境中托管和培养学生创业企业；大学为企业界提供办公空间、培训、资金和指导，为初创企业和各种规模的企业开发区域图表映射资源和联系

① European Investment Bank, 2019. *Investment Report 2019/2020 Accelerating Europe's Transformation*. Economics Department (EIB): 113.

② Ibid.

③ See: House of Commons-Canada, Standing Committee on Industry, Science and Technology, 2017. *Intellectual Property and Technology Transfer: Promoting Best Practices Report*, available at https://www.ourcommons.ca/Content/Committee/421/INDU/Reports/RP9261888/indurp08/indurp08-e.pdf, accessed 21 September 2020.

ment funds to those contributed by private sectors; development of student incubator; hosting and cultivating student start-up businesses in a collaborative environment; universities provide office space, training, funding, and mentoring to the business community; development of regional chart mapping resources and contacts for start-ups, and businesses of all sizes; development of universities' clinics where student clinicians empower small businesses and nonprofits by offering quality counseling, legal advice and representation, and community education information; development of an organization of career service professionals located in college-based and centralized career centers that connects students with internship and job opportunities.

In the end, financing of TTOs also depends on state policies about accessible funding, clear legal framework, available information, and developed evaluation mechanisms.

4.1.5 Scientific research

Discovery research is the process whereby private or government investment in the form of money is used to generate knowledge.① The effective TTO needs the existence of academic research achievements in various areas with potential for technology transfer application, and also needs financial resources for the scientific research. Quality scientific research is the base for TTO. Countries should be obliged to develop a strategy of finding and bringing new ideas into projects.

4.2 Organizational forms of TTO

TTOs exist in various organizational forms, but most TTOs exist as independent units or departments within the mother institution. The other organizational forms include an external company owned by or closely affiliated with the institution to manage its technology transfer activities; a service or consulting contract with a third-party company to manage occasional innovations disclosed by researchers; one office serving multiple institutions in a region under collaboration agreements, and a gov-

① See: Open Innovation available at http://www.faradaytechnology.com/Open_Innovation.htm, accessed 21 September 2020.

人；以及各种规模的业务发展大学诊所，让学生临床医生通过提供高质量的咨询、法律咨询和代理以及社区教育信息来增强小企业和非营利组织的能力；建立一个职业服务专业人员组织，该组织位于以大学为基础的集中职业中心，将学生与实习和就业机会联系起来。

最后，技术转移办公室的融资还取决于国家关于可获得资金、明确的法律框架、现有信息和发展的评估机制的政策。

4.1.5 科学研究

科学研究是指以货币形式进行的私人或政府投资被用来产生知识的过程[①]。有效的技术转移办公室需要有强大的科研领域的成果，具有技术转移应用的潜力，同时为科研提供财力。高质量科学研究是技术转移办公室的基础。各国有义务制定战略并在项目中寻找和提出新的想法。

4.2 技术转移办公室的组织形式

技术转移办公室以各种组织形式存在，但大多数技术转移办公室是作为母体机构内的独立单位或部门存在的。其他组织形式包括：由该机构拥有或与其密切相关的外部公司管理其技术转移活动；与第三方公司签订服务或咨询合同，以管理研究人员偶然的创新披露；根据合作协议为一个区域的多个机构提供服务的一个办公室，以及为一个区域、州或国家的大学

① See: Open Innovation available at http://www.faradaytechnology.com/Open_Innovation.htm, accessed 21 September 2020.

ernment agency serving as a TTO for universities and other research organizations in a region, state, or nation.① We can conclude that there are many examples of organizational forms of TTO. But, essential for the organizational forms of TTO is that its organizational design has to be collaborative with the activities TTO performs. Additionally, as TTO expands, they diversified to create individual operating divisions to manage focused tasks.②

The big question is, "Which is the best organizational form of TTO" Research institution has to pick the structure that best meets its needs. According to Terry A. Young (2007), Director of Research Development, University of South Dakota, USA, the closer the TTO is physical to the scientists and researchers it serves, the more effective it will be.③ He stresses that even in today's world of digital communication, none of the digital techniques can replace frequent face-to-face communication needed between the TTO staff and its inventors, or the ability to call, on short notice, meetings between project stakeholders, inventors, TTO staff, academic administrators, potential licensees, and so forth.④ In line with this, but having regard to all the circumstances of today's way of living and working, as well as the conditions in which younger generations grow and develop, we consider that, again, everything depends on the needs of the research institution and the TTO team.

---

① Young, A.T., 2007. Establishing a Technology Transfer Office, In Intellectual Property Management in Health and Agricultural Innovation: A Handbook of Best Practices (eds. A Krattiger, RT Mahoney, L Nelsen, et al.). MIHR: Oxford, U.K., and PIPRA: Davis, U.S.A:555.

② Ibid.

③ Ibid.

④ Ibid.

和其他研究组织提供技术转移服务的政府机构[①]。由此可以得出，技术转移办公室的组织形式有许多。但是，对于技术转移办公室的组织形式来说，至关重要的是它的组织设计必须与技术转移办公室协作执行。此外，随着技术转移办公室的扩展和多样化，通常要创建单独的业务部门来管理重点突出的任务[②]。

哪一种技术转移办公室组织形式最合适？研究机构必须选择最符合其需要的形式，技术转移办公室与它所服务的科学家和研究人员在社交距离上越接近，它就越有效[③]。即使在当今数字通信的世界中，任何数字技术都不能取代技术转移办公室工作人员与其发明者之间经常性的面对面交流，或者能够在短时间内召集项目利益相关者、发明者、技术转移办公室工作人员、学术管理人员、潜在被许可方等之间的会议[④]。据此并考虑到当今生活和工作方式的所有情况，以及年轻一代成长和发展的条件，我们仍然认为，一切都取决于研究机构和技术转移办公室团队的合作。

① Young, A.T., 2007. Establishing a Technology Transfer Office, In Intellectual Property Management in Health and Agricultural Innovation: A Handbook of Best Practices (eds. A Krattiger, RT Mahoney, L Nelsen, et al.). MIHR: Oxford, U.K., and PIPRA: Davis, U.S.A:555.

② Ibid.

③ Ibid.

④ Ibid.

5 TECHNOLOGY TRANSFER —POLICIES AND PROCEDURES

Each TTO works with researchers to turn their innovations into market opportunities that can benefit society.

TheTTOs' websites provide detailed information regarding the technology transfer process, policies connected to the technology transfer process, procedures and forms. There are many types of agreements and contracts, including grants, industry research agreements, licensing agreements, service agreements, letters of agreement, memoranda of understanding, purchase orders, and letters of intent.

The code of conduct for university staff appeared as the main contents of the website of TTO; university research integrity policy; intellectual property policy; national policy statement on ensuring research integrity; equality and diversity policy; policy for private consultancy, external commercial work and clinical research policy; facility use policy; equity interest and/or private business participation policy.

The forms and procedures related to the process of TT usually appear as the content of the website of the TTO. It includes the form of disclosure of the invention and work, one - way and mutual confidential agreement, the agreement of the pre - approved material transfer, the simple letter of agreement of material transfer, the procedure of misconduct accusation in the process of management and research, the conflict of interest, the procedure of the review of a research center, the authorization of proposal, the financial statements and recruitment of research, the disclosure

第五章　技术转移的政策和程序

技术转移办公室必须与研究人员密切合作，并将他们的创新转化为能够造福社会的市场机会。

技术转移办公室提供了关于技术转移过程，与技术转移过程有关的政策、程序、形式、协议和合同的详细信息。其中，协议和合同有多种类型，包括捐款、行业研究协议、许可协议、服务协议、协议书、谅解备忘录、定购单和意向书等。

技术转移办公室的网站经常包括针对工作人员的大学行为守则，大学研究诚信政策，知识产权政策，关于确保研究诚信的国家政策声明，平等和多样性政策，私人咨询政策、外部商业工作和临床研究政策，设施使用政策，股权和私营企业参与政策。

技术转移办公室网站通常也包含与技术转移过程有关的形式和程序，包括发明披露形式、工作形式披露、单向保密披露协议、相互保密披露协议、预先批准的材料转移协议、材料转移简易信函协议、管理研究中不当行为指控的程序、利益冲突、研究中心审查程序、提案授权表、研究财务表、研究招聘、知识产权披露表、学生专利和版权、在项目早期阶段撰写

of intellectual property, the patents and copyrights of the students, strategies to protect patents when writing proposals in the early stages of the project, the standard agreements of research, use the agreements of the use of facility or equipment, the agreements of the material transfer and confidentiality agreements.

Three types of agreements that are often involved in relationships between the university and industry are research agreements, service agreements and confidentiality agreements.

5.1 Research agreement

A research agreement is an agreement between university and external parties which determines core principles which are obligatory in this university–external party correlations. These principles generally relate to the following aspects, including the identity of the company, the scope of the work, the rights to know the confidential information, data and reports, the publishing policy, the control policy of the cost of facilities and administration, the payment, the research involving human subject policy, research involving animal policy, invention and patent, compensation, termination and application of the law. These principles are the foundation of all rights and obligations connected to the research results in the future.

5.1.1 Scope of work

The work scope is a detailed written description of the work to be undertaken by the principal researchers during the contract's performance. It must be clearly expressed and easy to understand. This scope of work is usually included as an attachment to the research agreement.

The issues associated with the research are developed and regulated in accordance with the applicable law, which is usually appropriate country's law.

In view of this, it should be noted that usually research involving human subjects and research involving animals is regulated with particular university policies that must be in accordance with the appropriate country's law.

5.1.2 Confidential information

University and external parties should define what confidential information is. It

建议书时保护专利保护的战略、标准研究协议、设施或设备使用协议、材料转移协议、保密协议。

大学和行业之间最常用的三种协议是：研究协议、服务协议和保密协议。

5.1 研究协议

研究协议是大学与外部各方之间的协议，它决定了这所大学必须遵守的核心原则。这些原则通常涉及公司身份、工作范围、机密信息、数据和报告中的权利、出版政策、设施和行政成本政策、支付，涉及人类主题政策的研究，涉及动物政策的研究、发明和专利、赔偿、终止和适用法律。这些原则是与未来研究成果有关的所有权利和义务的基础。

5.1.1 工作范围

工作范围是主要研究人员在合同履行期间将承担的工作的详细书面说明。它必须清楚地表达出来，易于理解，工作范围通常作为研究协议的附件。研究与之相关的整个问题都是根据国家法律的适用法律的发展和规范。通常涉及人类学科的研究和涉及动物的研究都是用特殊的大学政策来规范的，这也必须符合适应的国家法律。

5.1.2 机密信息

大学和相关方应该定义什么是机密信息。它可以是机密的科学、商业

could be confidential scientific, business, or financial information. It can also be defined very extensively or specifically, but it is desirable to be defined suitably in the case that not every piece of information is confidential, and it depends on every separate case. In our opinion, defining the borders for using the information, the obligation for every party to respect what has been agreed on the confidential information, and prescribed penalties for breach of this agreement should be an obligatory part of the agreement. TTO usually agrees to protect proprietary interest information and materials. TTO also enters into confidentiality contracts for the protection of its own proprietary information as well as the innovation itself. TTO is obliged not to disclose previously described information.

Regarding this, it should be mentioned that all the participants of the technology transfer process (researchers, staff, students, third parties) may be asked to sign a mutual or one-way agreement before receiving confidential information or before disclosing potentially confidential information.①

5.1.3 Rights in data and reports

University and external parties should agree about the rights in data and reports. Usually, all rights in data and materials from the university belong to the university. Regarding the university-industry technology transfer, the company is an inevitable part of the process as well as materials and data jointly developed by the company and university, under a contract. In these cases, the question about the owner of the copyrightable materials and data arises. As previously in this text described, there is no one-sized solution to this question. However, the university has an obligation to prevent data, information and material of researchers and research in an effective way, i.e., the data, information and material related to the research should be accessible for academic staff and scientific validation, but at the same time, they should be secured for the commercial partner too. It can lay the foundation for independent research and faculty but in accordance with the technology transfer process's demands. Therefore, the university enables its company partners to have insight into

① See: Cleveland State University. Technology Transfer Office Forms, available at https://www.csuohio.edu/technology-transfer/tech-transfer-forms, accessed 23 September 2020.

或财务信息。它也可以定义得非常广泛或具体。但在某种意义上，最好是适当地定义，不是每一项都是机密信息，它取决于每一种单独的情况。我们认为，在界定使用信息的边界时，每一方都有义务尊重与机密信息有关的协议以及对违反本协议的规定的处罚，这应是协议的强制性部分。技术转移办公室通常同意保护专有利益信息和材料。技术转移办公室还应签订保密合同，以保护自己的专有信息以及创新本身，且有义务不披露先前描述的信息。

关于这一点，应该提到的是，技术转移过程的所有参与者（研究人员、工作人员、学生、第三方）可能被要求在收到机密信息之前或在披露潜在的机密信息之前签署共同或单向协议[①]。

5.1.3　数据和报告中的权利

大学和相关方应就数据和报告中的权利达成一致。通常，来自大学的数据和材料的所有权利都属于大学。在大学—产业的技术转移中，公司以及由公司和大学根据合同共同开发的材料和数据是不可避免的环节。在这些情况下，出现了关于可版权材料和数据所有者的问题。正如前文所述的，这个问题没有一个详细的解决方案。然而，大学有义务以有效的方式保护研究人员和研究人员的数据、信息和材料的安全。与研究有关的数据、信息和材料应可供学术人员查阅和科学验证，但同时也应为商业伙伴确保这些数据、信息和材料。这可以为独立的研究和教师提供基础，但符合技术转移过程的要求。因此，大学使其公司合作伙伴能够

① See：Cleveland State University. Technology Transfer Office Forms，available at https://www.csuohio.edu/technology-transfer/tech-transfer-forms，accessed 23 September 2020.

the research process, and to use data, information and materials, but these rights are restricted and under special terms.

5.1.4 Publication policy

Scientific research is essentially connected to the publication. It affects the authors' reputation and the university's reputation. However, it should be understood that the freedom to publish research and its results is limited when it comes to the technology transfer process. Consequently, publication policy is a very important component of the university-industry agreements. This part of the agreement defines the opportunities for publication of the research and its results. Some TTOs have decided on the following solution: short delay (30 to 60 days) of the publication with the aim sponsor to review publications and to remove confidential information or establish patent protection before the results are released to the public.[①]

In addition, the owner of publication rights should be clearly defined. Usually, universities and authors have the right to reveal the fact that research exists, what its subject is and other general information, but never details.

5.1.5 Direct and indirect costs, and payment

Research is associated with costs of two types: direct and indirect costs. Direct costs can be explicitly identified (e.g., salaries, equipment for the research and travel expenses), while indirect costs are not directly associated with the research but are part of the research development (e.g., administrative support, utilities). Providing funds for the development of desired research and adequate cost management during the technology transfer process is also a challenging part of the process. Therefore, it is highly recommended that the universities have a cost methodology for the research and the research pieces.

Another question connected to the costs is the question about payment and time of payment. These questions are regulated by payment provisions as a part of the agreement. The first payment is usually requested at the time the agreement is signed and needs to be received before the project begins so that the university can be as-

① See: Cleveland State University. Technology Transfer Office Forms, available at https://www.csuohio.edu/technology-transfer/tech-transfer-forms, accessed 23 September 2020.

洞察研究过程，并使用数据、信息和材料，但这些权利在特殊条款下受到限制。

5.1.4 出版政策

科学研究大多数都与出版有关，出版物影响着作者的声誉和大学的声誉。但是，在技术转移过程中，发表研究成果的自由是有限的，这是可以理解的。因此，出版政策是大学—行业协议中的一个非常重要的组成部分。这部分协议确定了发表研究及其结果的机会。一些技术转移办公室已经决定了以下解决方案：出版物的短期延迟（30至60天），目的是赞助人在向公众发布结果之前审查出版物并删除机密信息或建立专利保护①。

此外，应明确界定出版权的所有者。通常，大学和作者有权揭示研究存在的事实，研究的主题和其他一般信息，但绝不是细节。

5.1.5 直接费用和间接费用及支付

研究与直接成本和间接成本有关。直接成本是指那些可以明确确定的成本（例如薪金、研究设备、差旅费）。间接成本是指那些与研究没有直接联系的成本，但它们是研究开发的一部分（例如：行政支出、公用事业）。在技术转移过程中为发展所需的研究和适当的成本管理提供资金也是这一进程的一个挑战。因此，强烈建议大学对研究和研究的部分采用成本计算方法。

与费用有关的另一个问题是关于付款和付款时间的问题。这些问题由作为协议一部分的付款规定加以规定，第一笔付款通常是在签署协议时要求的，需要在项目开始前收到，这样大学就可以保证有足够的项目资金来

① See: Cleveland State University. Technology Transfer Office Forms, available at https://www.csuohio.edu/technology-transfer/tech-transfer-forms, accessed 23 September 2020.

sured of adequate project funding to cover project expenses as they are incurred.① In regards to the other payments, they are also negotiated and agreed by the parties: monthly or another way as agreed. The final agreement about payment provisions must be in favor of greater use of payment for research② and ought to secure adequate development of the research.

5.2 Service agreement

A service agreement is a contract which is more business-like and usually relates to indirect costs. TTO uses this contract to regulate certain types of business relationships. For example, if there are some services connected to the research needed by the industry partner and are not included as indirect costs, TTO uses this kind of contract.

The main terms of service agreements are the following: clearly defined needed service, clearly defined how the services fit research, clearly identified how the services fit within the university's mission. For example, the subject of the service agreement may be an exclusive occasion for teaching and learning for faculty and students. Other contractual terms of this agreement are very similar to contractual terms of any other contract like detailed specifications of service, dates of services, cost and payment terms, liability, indemnification, address for notice for both sides, means of communication, termination.

5.2.1 Inventions and IP protection

Inventions and IP protection are closely related, and this interaction is essential for the technology transfer process and TTO. As previously concluded, ID plays a crucial role in the achievement of technology transfer process and TTO's activities and goals. As a consequence, a number of universities oblige all university employ-

① Ibid.

② See: The Norwegian National Research Ethics Committees, 2016. Payment of Research Subjects, available at https://www.forskningsetikk.no/en/resources/the-research-ethics-library/data-protection-and-responsibility-concerning-the-individual/payment-of-research-subjects/, accessed 22 September 2020.

支付项目费用[①]。关于其他付款，也由双方谈判和商定：每月或其他方式商定。关于支付条款的最终协议必须有利于更多地利用支付进行研究，并应确保研究的充分发展[②]。

5.2 服务协议

服务协议是一种商业合同，通常涉及间接成本。技术转移办公室使用本合同规范某些类型的业务关系，例如，一些与研究有关的服务、行业伙伴的需要、其他间接成本等。

服务协议的主要条款如下：明确界定所需服务，明确界定服务如何适合研究，明确确定服务如何适合大学使命。例如，服务协议的主题可能是教师教学和学生学习的主体活动。该协议的其他合同条款与任何其他合同的合同条款非常相似，如：详细的服务规格、服务日期、费用和付款条件、责任、赔偿、双方通信地址、通信手段和终止条款。

5.2.1 发明和知识产权保护

发明和知识产权保护密切相关，这种联系对于技术转移进程和技术转移至关重要。如前所述，发明披露在实现技术转移进程和技术转移办公室活动和目标方面发挥着关键作用。因此，一些大学要求允许使用大学研究设施的所有大学员工、非居民员工和访客披露大学在就业期间构思或开发

① Ibid.

② See: The Norwegian National Research Ethics Committees, 2016. Payment of Research Subjects, available at https://www.forskningsetikk.no/en/resources/the-research-ethics-library/data-protection-and-responsibility-concerning-the-indivual/payment-of-research-subjects/, accessed 22 September 2020.

ees, non-resident employees and visitors are permitted to use university research facilities, to disclose all inventions or discoveries conceived or developed while employed by the university, whether the research is funded by the university or by external sponsors.① This document is called Patent Acknowledgement Contract and is justified with the fact that the development and commercialization of invention may provide significant public benefit and generate income for research and education at university.② Actually, university, as previously mentioned develops IP protection policy, most often patent policy. The intent is to help all the parties in the technology transfer process to benefit IPRs protection. The commercial partner or sponsor of the research has the right to negotiate a commercial license.③

5.2.2 Compensation for harm or loss

The research, in view of its nature is risky. Consequently, all the parties-participants in the university-industry technology transfer process should be aware and should accept this actuality not as a limitation, but as an opportunity. On the other hand, this doesn't mean that universities and researchers do not have obligations: they are obliged to conduct research in the most appropriate manner for gaining the expected success. Thus, most universities will agree to indemnify the research sponsor but only for the willful misconduct or negligent conduct of university participants.

5.2.3 Termination of the agreement

As for the termination of the agreement, the prevailing rule is that any of the parties may terminate the agreement. But these situations are not unconditional.

①See: University of California State Oath of Allegiance. Patent Policy, and Patent Acknowledgment available at https://ucnet.universityofcalifornia.edu/forms/pdf/upay-585.pdf, accessed 22 September 2020; University of California, UC Office of President. UC Patent Acknowledgment, available at https://ucnet.universityofcalifornia.edu/compensation-and-benefits/patent-acknowledgment/, accessed 22 September 2020; Yale University Office of Cooperative Research.

② See: University of California San Francisco. Office of Technology Management, available at https://innovation.ucsf.edu/office-technology-management-faqs#Ive-made-a-discovery-Should-I-submit-an-invention-disclosure-form, accessed 22 September 2020.

③See: University of California San Francisco. Office of Technology Management, available at https://innovation.ucsf.edu/office-technology-management-faqs#Ive-made-a-discovery-Should-I-submit-an-invention-disclosure-form, accessed 22 September 2020.

的所有发明或发现，无论这项研究是由大学资助还是由外部赞助者资助①。本文件称为《专利确认合同》，其原因是发明的开发和商业化可能为大学的研究和教育提供重大的公共利益和创收②。事实上，正如前面提到的，大学制定了知识产权保护政策，最常见的是专利政策。目的是帮助技术转移过程中的各方为知识产权保护服务。研究的商业合作伙伴或发起人有权协商商业许可③。

5.2.2 损害或损失的赔偿

鉴于研究是有风险的，大学—产业技术转移过程中的所有参与者都应该意识到并接受这种现状，将其作为是一种机会，而不是一种限制。但这并不意味着大学和研究人员没有义务，他们有义务以最适当的方式进行研究，以获得预期的成功。因此，大多数大学将同意赔偿研究赞助人，但仅限于大学参与者的故意不当行为或疏忽行为。

5.2.3 终止协议

协议终止的通行规则是，任何一方都可以终止协议。但是，这些情况不是无条件的，即：各方当事人均可因合理原因终止协议，双方意见应在协议中明确，如果任何一方确定研究项目在学术、技术或商业上不再可

① See: University of California State Oath of Allegiance. Patent Policy, and Patent Acknowledgment available at https://ucnet.universityofcalifornia.edu/forms/pdf/upay-585.pdf, accessed 22 September 2020; University of California, UC Office of Pres ent. UC Patent Acknowledgment, available at https://ucnet.universityofcalifornia.edu/compensation-and-benefits/patent-acknowledgment/, accessed 22 September 2020; Yale University Office of Cooperative Research.

② See: University of California San Francisco. Office of Technology Management, available at https://innovation.ucsf.edu/office-technology-management-faqs#Ive-made-a-discovery-Should-I-submit-an-invention-disclosure-form, accessed 22 September 2020.

③ See: University of California San Francisco. Office of Technology Management, available at https://innovation.ucsf.edu/office-technology-management-faqs#Ive-made-a-discovery-Should-I-submit-an-invention-disclosure-form, accessed 22 September 2020.

Namely, each of the parties may terminate the agreement because of the reasonable cause, which in our opinion should be defined in the agreement. If any of the parties determines that the research project is no longer academically, technically or commercially feasible, the provider has the right to terminate the agreement, upon thirty days prior written notice to the other party.① When it comes to the termination of the agreement, the following up question is about financial losses resulting from termination. Again, a number of agreements contains provisions that the sponsor will be expected to reimburse the university for all project costs incurred to the date of termination and for all noncancellable and reasonable obligations uncancellable obligations.②

5.3 Confidentiality agreement

As previously mentioned, all the participants of the technology transfer process (researchers, staff, students, third parties) may be asked to sign a mutual or one-way agreement before receiving confidential information or before disclosing potentially confidential information. A confidentiality agreement is a legally binding agreement with the aim to protect the confidential information of the agreement parties. It typically obliges each of the parties to not disclose confidential information, but it also appears as one-way agreements depending on the situation. However, this agreement is and should be in favor of the university as well as the industry or business partner, which both have interests in protecting their proprietary and confidential

① See: University of Southern California, Sponsored Research Agreement available at https://research.usc.edu/files/2016/08/USC-Standard-Research-Agreement-8-24.pdf, accessed 23 September 2020; University of California UCDAVIS Office of Research. Research Agreements, available at https://research.ucdavis.edu/industry/partner-with-uc-davis/building-u-i-collaborations/research-transactions/types-agreements/research-agreements, accessed 23 September 2020 /; World Intellectual Property Organization.

② See: University of Maryland Office of Research Administration. Model Agreements, available at https://ora.umd.edu/resources/model-agreement, accessed 23 September 2020; University of California UCDAVIS Office of Research. Research Agreements, available at https://research.ucdavis.edu/industry/partner-with-uc-davis/building-u-i-collaborations/research-transactions/types-agreements/research-agreements, accessed 23 September 2020 /; World Intellectual Property Organization.

行，则提供方有权在提前三十天书面通知另一方时终止协议[①]。当涉及协议的终止时，后续问题是由于终止而造成的经济损失。同样，许多协议规定，要求主办人偿还大学截至终止之日发生的所有项目费用以及所有不可取消和合理的债务[②]。

5.3 保密协议

如前所述，技术转移过程的所有参与者（研究人员、工作人员、学生、第三方）可能被要求在收到机密信息之前或在披露潜在的涉密信息之前签署相互或单向协议。保密协议是一项具有法律约束力的协议，旨在保护协议各方的机密信息。它通常要求每一方不披露机密信息。保密协议应该有利于大学以及行业或商业伙伴保护他们的专有和机密的技术、研究和商业信息。

---

① See: University of Southern California, Sponsored Research Agreement available at https://research.usc.edu/files/2016/08/USC-Standard-Research-Agreement-8-24.pdf, accessed 23 September 2020; University of California UCDAVIS Office of Research. Research Agreements, available at https://research.ucdavis.edu/industry/partner-with-uc-davis/building-u-i-collaborations/research-transactions/types-agreements/research-agreements, accessed 23 September 2020 /; World Intellectual Property Organization.

② See: University of Maryland Office of Research Administration. Model Agreements, available at https://ora.umd.edu/resources/model-agreement, accessed 23 September 2020; University of California UCDAVIS Office of Research. Research Agreements, available at https://research.ucdavis.edu/industry/partner-with-uc-davis/building-u-i-collaborations/research-transactions/types-agreements/research-agreements, accessed 23 September 2020 /; World Intellectual Property Organization.

technical, research and business information.

Depending on the nature of the research and expected results, but also because of other justified reasons, a confidentiality agreement may be a mandatory step before any other joint activity.

A confidentiality agreement is also called a confidential disclosure agreement (CDA), a non-disclosure agreement (NDA) or a secrecy agreement.

It is advisable for researchers and other university staff involved in the technology transfer process to consult TTO about any questions, concerns and discussions related to this kind of agreement.

根据研究的性质和预期结果及其他正当理由，保密协议可能是任何其他联合活动之前的强制性步骤。

保密协议又称保密披露协议（CDA）、非披露协议（NDA）或保密协议。

参与技术转移进程的研究人员和其他大学工作人员应当就与这类协议有关的问题、关注点和意见向技术转移办公室咨询和沟通。

6 TECHNOLOGY TRANSFER — METRICS AND BENCHMARKS

The issue of what indicators, measures and processes are the most appropriate in order to measure the effectiveness of technology transfer and TTOs remains quite challenging and in a way under-researched worldwide.

6.1 Organization for Economic Cooperation and Development

In regards to the measurement of the technology transfer effectiveness, OECD identifies four fundamental problems of the organizations:[①]

• Timing: considered as the time gap between finished research and effects on society;

• Attribution: crediting some portion of impact to the sources used in developing a new innovation;

• Appropriability: the difficulty in identifying all parties affected by the research and

• Inequality: skewed results from the lack of attention to contrasts in project size; most effects are ascribed to large-scale research.

① OECD. 2006. *OECD Science, Technology, and Industry Outlook*. Paris: OECD Publishing.

第六章　技术转移的指标和基准

衡量技术转移和技术转移的有效性时，什么样的指标、措施和程序是最合适的，这一问题在世界范围内仍然是一个相当具有挑战性的问题，而且在某种程度上还没有得到充分的研究。

6.1 经济合作与发展组织

关于技术转移实效的衡量，经合组织（OECD）确定了四个基本问题[①]：

• 时机：完成研究与对社会产生影响之间的时间间隔；

• 归因：将某些影响部分计入开发新创新所用的资源；

• 适用性：能够衡量研究和影响的所有方面；

• 不平等性：由于缺乏对项目规模对比的关注而产生的扭曲结果，大多数影响归因于大规模的研究。

① OECD. 2006. *OECD Science, Technology, and Industry Outlook*. Paris: OECD Publishing.

6.2 MIT Skoltech Initiative

In the study of *Creating university - based entrepreneurial ecosystems evidence from emerging world leader*① *indicators* about the entrepreneurship and innovation capabilities of the universities are divided into three main groups: input indicators, process indicators and output indicators. This study uses quantitative along with qualitative data.

Input indicators relate to the university strategy, policies and activities in correlation with the knowledge transfer and entrepreneurship and innovation, as well as education and development opportunities like offered curricula and training devoted to entrepreneurship and innovation.②

Process indicators relate to the entrepreneurial culture and innovation capacity within the university with an emphasis on the student and staff attitudes and aspirations like participation in voluntary entrepreneurship, career intentions and options, how many students are interested in joining entrepreneurship classes, connectivity between the university and industry (like web connectivity, joint publications, number of students who combine study with jobs with high-tech firms, number of university patents, but also free movement of faculty in and out of the university), the research quality and reputation of the university, faculty trust in the university TTO (or equivalent); a percentage of faculty engaged in disclosures/patenting activity.③ According to this study, the measurement of students and staff attitude, the entrepreneurial climate and intentions are important indicators for the entrepreneurial and innovation directions in the future.

Output indicators relate to the impact of the university on the ecosystem. This type of indicator contented in the study is the standard type of indicator. First, the number of TTO and the disclosed patents, the number of start-ups/spin-offs, and

① See: Ruth, G., 2014. *Creating University-based Entrepreneurial Ecosystems Evidence from Emerging World Leaders*, MIT Skoltech Initiative.

② Ibid.

③ Ibid.

6.2 麻省理工学院斯科尔科沃科学技术研究计划

在《从新兴世界领导人那里创造基于大学的创业生态系统证据》①的研究中，关于大学创业和创新能力的指标分为三组：投入指标、过程指标和产出指标。本研究使用定量和定性数据，即，麻省理工学院斯科尔科沃科学技术研究计划。

投入指标涉及大学战略、政策和与知识转移、创业和创新相关的活动以及教育和发展机会，如提供的创业和创新课程和培训等②。

过程指标涉及大学内的创业文化和创新能力，重点是学生和工作人员的态度和愿望，如参与自愿创业、职业意向和选择、有多少学生有兴趣参加创业课程、大学与产业之间的联系（如网络连接、联合出版物、将学习与工作与高科技公司结合起来的学生人数、大学专利数量，以及大学内外教师的自由流动）、大学的研究质量和声誉，教师对大学技术转移办公室（或）的信任；从事披露专利活动地教师百分比③。根据本研究对学生和员工态度的测量，创业氛围和内涵是未来创业和创新方向的重要指标。

产出指标涉及大学对生态系统的影响。研究中满足的这类指标是标准型指标。首先，技术转移办公室和披露专利的数量、初创企业和分拆企业

① See: Ruth, G., 2014. *Creating University-based Entrepreneurial Ecosystems Ev ibid dence from Emerging World Leaders*, MIT Skoltech Initiative.

② Ibid.

③ Ibid.

the number of licenses; second, the creation of sustainable companies related to the number and financial value of companies; third, the impact of university graduates, such as the connection between alumni or graduates and ecosystems; fourth, the view of ecosystems through the attitudes of people or universities in different opportunity regions. The broader development of integration and its impact on changing policies and the ratios of all start-ups and high-tech companies.①

6.3 Association of Public Land-Grant Universities

Institutions might consider the work of the Association of Public Land-Grant Universities—creating Economic Engagement Framework New Metrics Field Guide to measuring university contributions to the economy. This Guide uses quantitative data; and the relationship between universities and industry measures through the following metrics: sponsored research by industry, human clinical trials and service to external clients. Research metrics include the number of grants, contracts, sub-agreements, and sponsored research projects, number of individual private sector entities funding research grants and contracts, and dollar value of industry-sponsored research expenditures.② Human clinical trials measures include the number of active trials, number of subjects enrolled in clinical trials during the time period, number of protocols approved during the time period, number of trials initiated during the time period and dollar value of sponsored research grants for which clinical trials were conducted.③ Services to external clients include metrics such as the number of organizations served and the number of companies that provided on-site technical services.④ Besides the previously described measures, this Guide is in line with the conviction that there is no single metric as the answer for the measurement of technology transfer effectiveness, and provides additional metrics like umber of in-

① Ibid.

② Association of Public and Land-Grant Universities, 2014. *Economic Engagement Framework New Metrics Field Guide Measuring University Contributions to the Economy.*

③ Ibid.

④ Ibid.

的数量、许可证的数量；第二，创建与公司数量和财务价值相关的可持续公司；第三，大学毕业生的影响力，如：校友和毕业生与生态系统之间的联系；第四，通过不同机会的地区的人和大学的态度看待生态系统的更广泛发展及其对不断变化的政策以及所有初创企业和高科技公司的比率的影响①。

6.3 公共土地授予大学协会

技术转移办公室应当考虑到公共土地授予大学协会的工作，其制定的《经济参与框架新指标领域指南》能衡量大学对经济的贡献。这一指南使用定量数据，以及大学与行业之间的关系，通过以下指标衡量：由行业赞助的研究、人类临床试验和为外部客户提供服务。研究指标包括赠款、合同、次级协议、赞助的研究项目、资助研究赠款和合同的私营企业实体的数目，以及工业赞助的研究支出的美元价值②。人类临床试验措施包括积极试验的数量、在此期间参加临床试验的受试者的数量、在此期间批准的协议的数量、在此期间启动地试验的数量以及进行临床试验的赞助研究赠款的美元价值③。向外部客户提供的服务包括：服务的组织数目和提供现场技术服务的公司数目④。除上述措施外，该指南还符合以下信念，即没有单一的衡量标准作为衡量技术转移实效的答案，并提供了额外的衡量标

① Ibid.

② Association of Public and Land-Grant Universities, 2014. *Economic Engagement Framework New Metrics Field Guide Measuring University Contributions to the Economy*.

③ Ibid.

④ Ibid.

dustry consortia agreements, the dollar value of contracts received by institutions by type of guarantee organization, etc.[①]

6.4 Initiatives of governments

Governments of some countries have created initiatives for support and development of the technology transfer through funding agencies. This funding is associated with the assessment of the results, i.e., funded organizations are required to provide outcome reports.

It is obvious that these outcome reports are developed on the basis of some metrics. In respect of this, the technology transfer metrics used by most public research organizations in North America utilize quantitative data, and are divided into two categories: primary and secondary metrics. Primary metrics cover: number of invention disclosures, patent applications, executed licenses, formed start-up companies and total income from licenses.[②] Secondary metrics include: number of US-issued patents, active licenses, full-time professionals in TTOs, legal expenditures on the protection of IP, value of sponsored research expenditures and total income from royalties.[③]

6.5 Association of University Technology Managers

According to the AUTM, in addition to the traditional measures, some TTOs also consider these aspects of knowledge transfer:[④] the ability to attract and retain distinguished, entrepreneurial faculty, average faculty salary, ability to attract outstanding graduate students, and contribution to the institutional reputation for innovation. Actually, AUTM points out qualitative measures in line with quantitative

---

① Ibid.

② Gardner, P.L., Fong, A.Y. and Huang, R.L., 2010. Measuring the impact of knowledge transfer from public research organizations: a comparison of metrics used around the world. *International Journal of Learning and Intellectual Capital*, 7(3—4):318-327.

③ Ibid.

④ Association of University Technology Managers, 2007. The AUTM—Frequently Asked Questions, available at http://www.autm.net/aboutTT/aboutTT_faqs.cfm.

准，如行业联营集团协议的数目、按担保组织类型分列的机构收到的合同的美元价值等[①]。

6.4　政府的倡议

一些国家的政府通过供资机构制定了支持和发展技术转移的举措。这笔资金与评估结果有关。资助的组织必须提供结果报告[②]。

显然，这些成果报告是在一些指标的基础上编写的。在这方面，北美大多数公共研究组织使用的技术转移指标是定量数据，分为两类：主要指标和次要指标。主要指标包括发明披露的数量、专利申请、执行的许可证、成立的初创公司和许可证的总收入。次要指标包括美国颁发的专利数量、有效许可证、技术转移办公室的全职专业人员、保护知识产权的法律支出、赞助研究支出的价值和特许权使用费的总收入[③]。

6.5　大学技术管理人员协会

大学技术管理人员协会除了采取传统的措施外，技术转移办公室还考虑了知识转移的这些方面[④]：吸引和留住杰出员工的能力、平均员工工资的能力、吸引优秀研究生的能力以及对创新的机构声誉的贡献。

① Ibid.

② Gardner, P.L., Fong, A.Y. and Huang, R.L., 2010. Measuring the impact of knowledge transfer from public research organisations: a comparison of metrics used around the world. *International Journal of Learning and Intellectual Capital*, 7(3-4):318-327.

③ Ibid.

④ Association of University Technology Managers, 2007. The AUTM — Frequently Asked Questions, available at http://www.autm.net/aboutTT/aboutTT_faqs.cfm.

measures.

6.6 University Companies Association

The report of UNICO, Metrics for the Evaluation of Knowledge Transfer Activities at Universities[①], developed a framework of measures for the evaluation of knowledge transfer activities at UK universities. For this purpose, UNICO decided on quantity along with quality evaluation, i.e., the measures are divided into two main categories: measures of quantity and measures of quality. In this regard, UNICO firstly identifies mechanisms of knowledge: networks, continuing professional development, consultancy, collaborative research, contract research, licensing, spin-outs, teaching and the last mechanism is identified as other measures.

According to UNICO, if the universities respect described measures, the process of measurement and described steps, they can directly measure their knowledge transfer activities. In view of this, UNICO advises universities to be focused on directly measuring the knowledge transfer activities that they undertake.[②]

6.7 Measurement of the technology transfer efficiency in the literature — most challenging issues

Literature indicates different models and frameworks for measurement of the technology transfer efficiency and the efficiency of TTOs, founded first of all on quantity and monetary, but also on quality and non-monetary indicators. While literature develops various sets of measures, on the other hand, the literature lacks a standard set of measures as well as an internationally unified set of measures or indexes.

Regarding literature on the measurement of technology transfer, we emphasize the most challenging issues we believe should be considered when measuring the effi-

① UNICO. *Metrics for the Evaluation of Knowledge Transfer Activities at Universities*. Cambridge: Library House. http://ec.europa.eu/invest-in-research/pdf/download_en/library_house_2008_unico.pdf, accessed 23 September 2020.

② Ibid.

6.6 大学公司协会

英国大学公司协会在《评价大学知识转移活动的指标》[①]这一报告中制定了评价英国大学知识转移活动的措施架构，大学公司协会决定指标数量和质量评价。这些措施分为两大类：数量措施和质量措施。

国际信息和通信组织首先确定了知识机制：网络、持续专业发展、咨询、合作研究、合同研究、许可、分拆、教学，最终机制如何确定等其他措施。

国际信息和通信组织界定，如果大学尊重所描述的措施、测量过程和所描述的步骤，它们可以直接衡量其知识转移活动。有鉴于此，国际信息和通信组织建议各大学将重点放在直接衡量其开展的知识转移活动上[②]。

6.7 文献中技术转移效率的测量——最具挑战性的问题

文献表明，衡量技术转移效率和技术转移组织效率的不同模型和框架，首先是数量和货币，但也是质量和非货币指标。文献在改进各种措施的同时，但另一方面，文献缺乏一套标准的措施以及国际统一的措施或指标。

关于技术转移测量的文献，我们强调在测量技术转移的效率和技术转

① UNICO. *Metrics for the Evaluation of Knowledge Transfer Activities at Universities*. Cambridge: Library House. http://ec.europa.eu/invest-in-research/pdf/download_en/library_house_2008_unico.pdf, accessed 23 September 2020.

② Ibid.

ciency of the technology transfer and the TTOs' efficiency.

Langford et al. (2006) emphasize the issue with the indicators regarding the possibility for the indicators becoming the aim itself.① For example, one of the most often used measures is the number of patents a university or researchers apply: the bigger number of patents, the more efficient university or TTO. Using this measure may result only in the production of a number of patents instead of the principal patent function: protection of worthwhile IP.

Gardner et al. (2010) stress the question about mechanisms suitable to measure the quality and quantity of the measured results.② Namely, knowledge transfer activities differ in quality and quantity; they can be compared, but what about the mechanism suitable to measure the quality and quantity of the measured results. Their conclusion is that there is currently no such mechanism. For example, the number of spinoffs is also one of the commonly used measures for the evaluation of technology transfer process and TTO's efficiency. The problem is that this measurement does not include the rate of success of the spinoff or its commercial impact. Another example in line with this is about comparing institutions: some institutions may have few spinoffs, but with much more benefits for the society, that the institution which has a large number of spinoffs.

The huge amount of published literature on this topic indicates the importance of measuring technology transfer for all stakeholders, but on the other hand, providing practical performance assessments is still a significant challenge for all technology transfer stakeholders as well. Providing practical evaluations of effectiveness is a significant challenge for technology transfer professionals. The research confirms that different institutions use different quantitative indicators such as number of innovations, number of patents, the total number of licenses, number of active licenses,

① See: Langford, C.H., Hall, J., Josty, P., Matos, S. and Jacobson, A., 2006. Indicators and outcomes of Canadian university research: Proxies becoming goals? *Research policy*, 35(10): 1586-1598.

② See: Gardner, P.L., Fong, A.Y. and Huang, R.L., 2010. Measuring the impact of knowledge transfer from public research organizations: a comparison of metrics used around the world. *International Journal of Learning and Intellectual Capital*, 7(3-4):318-327.

让办公室的效率时，我们应该考虑最具挑战性的问题。

关于指标是否可能成为目标本身的指标问题[①]，最常用的衡量标准之一是大学或研究人员申请的专利数量，专利数量越多、效率越高的大学拥有技术转移办公室越多。使用这一措施可能只会产生数量的专利，而不是主要的专利功能也就是保护有价值的知识产权。

在适合测量结果质量和数量的机制的问题上[②]知识转移活动在质量和数量上存在差异，它们可以进行比较，但适合测量结果质量和数量的机制目前没有。例如，附带利益的数量也是评估技术转移过程和技术转移办公室效率的常用措施之一。这一措施不包括分拆的成功率或其商业影响。与此相一致的另一个例子是比较机构，一些机构可能没有多少附带利益，但对社会有更多的好处，即机构有大量附带利益。

大量研究文献表明，技术转移的衡量对所有利益攸关方至关重要，但是，提供实际业绩评估对所有技术转移利益攸关方来说仍然是一个艰巨的挑战，尤其是提供切实有效的评估方法。研究证实，不同的机构使用不同的量化指标，如：创新数量、专利数量、许可证总数、有效许可证数量、分公司数量、签订的研究合同数量、许可证总收入、技术转移办公室雇员

① See: Langford, C.H., Hall, J., Josty, P., Matos, S. and Jacobson, A., 2006. Indicators and outcomes of Canadian university research: Proxies becoming goals? *Research policy*, 35(10): 1586-1598.

②See: Gardner, P.L., Fong, A.Y. and Huang, R.L., 2010. Measuring the impact of knowledge transfer from public research organisations: a comparison of metrics used around the world. *International Journal of Learning and Intellectual Capital*, 7(3-4):318-327.

number of spinoff companies, number of research contracts concluded, total license revenue, number of employees in the TTO, the value of expenditure on sponsored research, etc. Considering the goal of indicators of assessing technology transfer and TTO's effectiveness, this would affect TTO funding in turn. It opens up the possibility of exaggerating the numbers and their significance, without attempting to create mechanisms for assessing the quantity, but also the quality of indicators and measured results. We argue that university - industry technology transfer can unfold in many ways and impact many stakeholders. Therefore, choosing indicators focused on a narrow range of activities and impacts, especially in highly differentiated university systems, might limit the ability of universities to represent their transfer technology performance accurately. In regard to this, not only indicators but also the question of methods and their structure is substantial. A primary method commonly used by organizations for collecting data is voluntary surveys only for their members, and dissemination of the results through annual reports. Additionally, the nature of data collected is crucial as well. Most often, this is quantitative data, but some organizations are taking steps to more abstract, subjective measures such as anecdotes and case studies.[①] For this reason, benchmarks for a TTO should include a variety of activities and reflect a variety of impacts so as to allow comparability between different institutions and avoid the creation of undesirable behavioral incentives. We believe this is a field for experimentation, but also an opportunity for making the future.

① Gardner, P.L., Fong, A.Y. and Huang, R.L., 2010. Measuring the impact of knowledge transfer from public research organizations: a comparison of metrics used around the world. *International Journal of Learning and Intellectual Capital*, 7(3-4):318-327.

人数、赞助研究支出价值等。这类指标的目标是评估技术转移和技术转移的有效性，这将反过来影响技术转移办公室的工资。它提供了夸大数字及其重要性的可能性，而没有试图建立评估数量的机制，也没有建立评估指标和衡量结果的质量的机制。我们认为，大学—产业技术转移可以在许多方面展开，并影响许多利益相关者。因此，选择侧重于范围狭窄的活动和影响的指标，特别是在高度差异化的大学系统中，可能会限制大学准确表示其转移技术绩效的能力。在这方面，指标和方法及其结构问题也很关键。各组织收集数据的主要方法是只对其成员进行自愿调查，并通过年度报告传播结果。此外，收集的数据的性质也至关重要。最常见的是定量数据，一些技术转移办公室正在采取步骤，采取更抽象、更主观的措施，如轶事和案例研究①。因此，技术转移办公室基准应包括各种活动，并反映各种影响，以便不同机构之间的进行比较，避免产生不良的行为激励。我们相信，这是一个实验领域，也是创造未来的机会。

① Gardner, P.L., Fong, A.Y. and Huang, R.L., 2010. Measuring the impact of knowledge transfer from public research organizations: a comparison of metrics used around the world. *International Journal of Learning and Intellectual Capital*, 7(3-4):318-327.

CONCLUSION

As a factor for economic development, innovation is conditioned by human capital. Without the development of human capital, there is no development of the economy. Universities are a basic environment for the development and promotion of human capital, i.e., innovation. Technology transfer is one of the major factors for strengthening the university capacities in order to develop activities in the field of innovation.

Recent trends in education systems globally show enhanced measures in the field of vocational training and retraining to meet the demands of the labor market, the needed staff qualifications, i.e., available and required skills, both in the private and public sector. Innovation goes one step further and plays a key role in strengthening a country's economy. Various regions across the world show the different presence of and commitment to the technology transfer. Countries with undeveloped technology transfers should follow the example of developed countries which invest in research and development along with technology transfer. This will result in strengthened university capacities with potential in innovative activities. Regarding this, different types of research studies, case studies with recommended mechanisms, methods and practices, which bring practical solutions to strengthen the innovative activities in higher education institutions, are needed.

For the purpose of this book, we first analyzed the process of technology trans-

结 论

作为经济发展的一个因素，创新受到人力资本的制约。没有人力资本的发展，就没有经济的发展。大学是开发人力资本，促进人力资本发挥效力的基本环境，也是通过创新技术转移推动大学职能的实现，激发其创新领域活动的主要因素之一。

全球教育系统最新发展趋势显示，为了满足劳动力市场的需求，职业培训和再培训领域的措施得到加强，如所需的员工职业资格，即私营和公共部门现有和所需的技能。创新在促进一个国家的经济发展方面发挥着关键作用。世界各国对技术转移的态度和承诺各不相同。技术转移不发达的国家应仿效发达国家投资研究和发展技术转移的做法，加强大学在创新活动方面的能力和潜力。鉴于此，我们需要进行不同类型的研究和案例分析，使用推荐的机制、方法和实践进行案例研究，为推动高等教育机构创新活动的开展提供切实可行的办法。

本书根据大学的技术转移实践，分析了发达国家和发展中国家的技术

fer in developed and developing countries with special reference to the universities that practice technology transfer. We started the analysis by defining the concept of technology transfer through the types of technology transfer and ended with an analysis of technology transfer between universities and the businesses and industry, which is of special interest to us. The technology transfer process is a set of several components: determination of new technologies; protection of technologies through intellectual property rights; development of commercialization strategies, such as marketing of new technologies, licensing, spinoffs or creating new technology-based companies. We found that the process of technology transfer always depends directly on the policies and values of each country and institution separately. The unequivocal conclusion is that established economic, political and social-cultural factors are of particular importance for the functioning and further development of technology transfer.

The research on the practical realization of technology transfer process imposed the problem of the management of the process. We have found that the management of the process especially managing the process of the commercialization of innovation, is a problem researched by many authors from different aspects, but still remains complex and in some aspects even unexplored, because this process throughout different institutions requires development of its own structural elements for gaining so required efficiency. These structural elements of the technology transfer process repent across different institutions, but still closely depend on a number of objective and subjective factors of the specific environment in which the process develops. Therefore, we have concluded that the positive experiences in this area can not only be copied. Instead, they should be researched and directions of good practice should be established as a base for the prediction of the impact of various factors on the technology transfer process. Due to these reasons, we first searched for the best model for managing innovation, through research and analysis of different data, strategic documents, contracts, studies of different management tactics, official legal documents and political acts and using literature and studies connected with the issue. Also, statistical data, information in the on-line resources and official websites

转移过程。先通过技术转移的类型来定义技术转移，后又对大学与企业和行业之间的技术转移进行了分析。技术转移过程由确定新技术、通过知识产权保护技术、制定商业化战略（如新技术的营销、许可、分拆或创造新的技术型公司）等部分组成。技术转移过程总是直接取决于每个国家和机构各自的政策和价值。也就是说，既定的经济、政治和社会文化因素对技术转移的运作和进一步发展特别重要。

对技术转移过程实际实现的研究，对过程管理问题也大有益处。我们发现，过程的管理，特别是创新商业化过程的管理，是许多学者从不同方面研究的问题，但仍然存在复杂且尚未探索的方面，因为这个过程需要不同机构发展自己的结构要素，才能获得必要的效率。技术转移过程的这些结构要素在不同的机构之间发挥作用，但仍与该过程发展的特定环境的一些客观和主观因素密切相关。由此，我们的结论是，这一领域的积极经验不能仅仅照搬照抄，应该研究这些经验，并确立良好做法的方向，为预测各种因素对技术转移过程的影响打下基础。因此，要通过研究和分析不同的数据、战略文件、合同、不同管理策略研究、官方法律文件和政治行为，以及可利用的相关文献和研究，寻找管理创新的最佳模式。此外，统计数据、在线资源信息以及不同技术转移办公室的官方网站也是定性和定量分析的对象。这部分研究旨在建立一种符合若干基本条件的创新管理模式和策略，在加强和发展大学创新活动能力方面发挥重要作用，对高校与企业、产业关系的发展和推动产生积极影响，使科研部门更接近学生，从

of different technology transfer offices were the subject of qualitative and quantitative analysis. This part of the research was aimed at establishing a model/tactic for innovation management that will meet several basic conditions: to play a significant role in strengthening and developing the capacity of innovation activities at the universities; to positively influence the development and promotion of the relations between the universities and the businesses and industry; to bring the real sector closer to the students, and thus to have an indirect and positive influence on the teaching performance and the preparation of the students; and finally, to have a positive impact on society as a whole because the end-users of innovation are the citizens. Through this part of the research, we found that the technology transfer offices meet the necessary requirements. Therefore, we dedicated the further part of the research to be dedicated to the structural elements for the successful establishment and functioning of the TTO; the practical experiences of TTO; TTO services and activities; links and impact of TTO on universities and external actors (primarily the business community) and vice versa; the overall contribution of the TTO role in the development of society as a whole; designing an efficient TTO model; determining and designing the entire documentation necessary for the successful functioning of the TTO and determining the elements for evaluating the success of the TTO.

Technology transfer offices are structures whose common key role is to assist universities in managing their innovations in a way that their services and activities will facilitate the transformation of innovations into social benefits, and the end result will be satisfying for all participants in the process: universities, innovators, TTO and citizens.

In order to be able to fulfill this basic function, the TTO has to carry out a series of activities. TTO activities are specific operations that correspond to the different stages of the technology transfer process and can be divided into three basic groups: innovation discovery, protection of innovation and commercialization. Each of these TTO activities has its own phases and sub-phases that enable a successful implementation of the specific activity. The activities of TTO occupy a significant part of the research and they are analyzed and presented in detail and in easy and

而间接地对学生的教学表现和准备产生积极影响，最后，因为创新的最终用户是公民，该研究还应对整个社会产生积极影响。通过这部分研究我们还发现了技术转移办公室应满足的必要条件。因此，我们的进一步研究主要致力于以下方面：成功建立和运作技术转移办公室的结构要素，技术转移办公室的实际经验，技术转移办公室的服务和活动，技术转移办公室与大学和外部行为者（主要是业界）的联系及相互产生的影响，技术转移办公室作用对整个社会发展的总体贡献，有效的技术转移办公室模式的设计，确定和设计技术转移办公室成功运作的必备资料，并确定评价技术转移办公室成功的要素。

技术转移办公室是一种结构，其关键作用是协助大学管理其创新，其服务和活动将促进创新转化为社会福利，最终结果将使所有参与这一进程的参与者（大学、创新者、技术转移办公室和公民）满意。

为了履行这一基本职能，技术转移办公室必须开展一系列活动。技术转移工作是对应于技术转移过程的不同阶段的具体操作，可分为三个基本组：创新发现、创新保护和商业化。每一项技术转移办公室的工作都有自己的阶段和分阶段，能够成功实施具体工作。技术转移办公室的工作占据了研究的重要部分，对其进行的详细分析和介绍使其更契合大学和商业部门。

simple ways in order to bring them closer to the universities and the business sector.

The establishment and successful functioning of TTO depends on a number of factors, among which a decisive influence has the following: the national economic strategy, which in a modern society should ensure that the technology transfer will be a long-term goal, and accordingly will enable the development of TTO; then, the intellectual property system of particular state or university which should be composed of clearly defined and transparent rules; and human resources with knowledge and skills necessary to ensure the successful implementation of the TTO activities.

Through detailed comparative analysis, we find that TTO has developed its own clearly defined, transparent, easy to access and easy to understand behavior strategy, and formed documents and procedures. On the one hand, it helps them to promote and get close to the academic personnel, innovators and business departments. On the other hand, the implementation of every activity tends to be easy. Of course, these policies, documents and procedures are in accordance with the legal order of the country and above all, they refer to the submission of innovation to the TTO, confidentiality, conflict of interests, patent procedures and forms of licensing.

One of the hardest obstacles in the development of TTO is the lack of the necessary funding from public and private funds. The comparative analysis has clearly shown that the finances provided by the countries in various ways, aimed to demonstrate the commercial potential of the academic environment in order to enable the innovation to enter the market, are insufficient both in terms of the amount and in view of the duration for which those funds are provided. This conclusion is unequivocal for the developed and less developed countries. The recommendations in this regard are to increase the number of state funds in order to mitigate the risks for the TTO activities. The recommendations include the issuance of so-called commercialization coupons, with the sole purpose of financing technology transfer activities; further, a mandatory percentage of state-allocated funds to be allocated for the universities to support research and technology transfer activities; as well as financial support to enterprises, which would include programs for financing technology transfer development initiatives, through various development programs.

技术转移办公室的建立和成功运作取决于若干因素，其中具有决定性影响的因素是国家经济战略。在现代社会中，国家经济战略应确保技术转移是一项长期目标，并有助于技术转移办公室的发展。此外，特定国家或大学的知识产权制度应由明确界定的、透明的规则组成；人力资源应具有确保技术转移办公室工作成功实施所必需的知识和技能。

通过详细的比较分析，我们发现技术转移办公室制定了自己明确透明、易于获取和理解的行为策略，形成文件和程序。一方面帮助他们提高水平，了解学术人员、创新者和业务部门，另一方面便于实施每项活动。当然，这些政策、文件和程序符合国家的法律秩序，最重要的是，它们涉及向技术组织提交创新、保密、利益冲突、专利程序和许可形式等内容。

技术转移办公室发展的最大障碍之一是缺乏来自公共和私人基金的必要资金。比较分析清楚地表明，为了展示学术环境的商业潜力，使创新能够进入市场，各国以各种方式提供资金，但是在资金数额和资金期限方面通常都不能完全满足需求。这一结论在发达国家和较不发达国家来说是明确的，因此，这方面的建议是增加国家资金数额，以减轻技术转移办公室活动的风险。比如发放商业化优惠券以资助技术转移活动。此外，为大学确定分配国家拨款的强制性百分比，以支持研究和技术转移活动，给企业的财政支持来资助技术转移项目发展。

Research has shown that the establishment and development of TTOs result in a number of benefits for the universities, industry, business sector, but also for the society and the region. These benefits are causally related to the TTO activities. The analysis of the activities of the TTO indicates a number of direct benefits provided by the existence and functioning of the TTO, for example, TTOs regularly have the capacity to meet the requirements set by the law of the particular state during all stages of the technology transfer process, to follow the whole process of commercialization in all its phases and to provide the necessary assistance; regularly and timely process the contracts required at each stage of the innovation commercialization process; TTO allows bridging the gap between academia and industry/business sector, encouraging the business sector to participate in research and vice versa; promotes the availability of innovation to the public; encourages the growth of innovation and the success of researchers; improves the university's rating; promotes cooperation between the private sector and research institutions and facilitates their relationships; ensures that all participants, the university, the researcher and the enterprise, will receive sufficient rights and financial benefits from the commercialization of the innovation; ensures minimization of costs for the technology transfer process and maximization of its pragmatic perspective; generates interest in investing in new research areas by providing subsequent benefits or improvements in research funding; provides assistance in applying for innovation support programs; acts as a service center for the university, staff and students in all areas related to intellectual property, including the consulting services.

One of the most significant benefits of TTO is its impact on the economy. Research has shown that a university with a TTO will have a higher expected number of patents than a university without a TTO, and the effect of having a TTO is increasing over time.

Investing in TTO activities results in several types of "returning" on the invested: reinvesting the research itself, creating new jobs and a new product or service for public benefit. There is no doubt that business benefits from technology in the modern world, but universities and the enterprise should see TTO as a place where

研究表明，技术转移办公室的建立和发展为大学、产业、商业部门和社会带来了许多好处。这些好处与技术转移办公室活动有直接的因果关系。对技术办公室活动的分析表明了技术办公室存在和运作的直接好处，例如，技术转移办公室在技术转移过程的所有阶段都有能力满足特定国家法律规定的要求，在所有阶段都遵循商业化进程并提供必要的援助，能够定期和及时地处理创新商业化进程的每一阶段所需的合同。技术转移办公室便于缩小学术界与产业/商业部门之间的差距，鼓励商业部门参与研究。技术转移办公室还能促进创新向公众开放，鼓励创新的增长和研究人员的成功，提高大学的评级，促进私营企业和研究机构之间的合作并促进它们之间的关系，确保所有参与者，即大学、研究人员和企业，从创新的商业化中获得足够的权利和经济利益，确保技术转移过程的成本最小化，实用性最大化。此外，还可通过提供后续研究资金或改进措施，产生对新研究领域投资的兴趣，协助申请创新支持方案，在与知识产权及其咨询服务有关的所有领域为大学、工作人员和学生充当服务中心。

技术转移办公室最大的好处之一是它对经济的影响。研究表明，拥有技术转移办公室的大学比没有技术转移办公室的大学拥有更高的预期专利数量，而且随着时间的推移，拥有技术转移办公室的效果还在增加。

对技术转移办公室的投资产生了投资的几种“回报”类型，如对研究本身的再投资，出于公共利益创造新的就业机会和新的产品或服务。毫无疑问，在现代世界，商业受益于技术，而大学和企业应该把技术转移办公室看作是一个他们可以共同创造未来的地方。技术转移办公室是一种间接

they can create the future together. TTO is a tool that indirectly unleashes university and business potential to contribute to economic growth, social progress and cultural development. So, when you think and discuss TTO, think about the impact TTO has on the local level, but also around the world.

The question of which indicators are the most appropriate for measuring the effectiveness of technology transfer and TTOs in technology transfer activities remains relatively under-researched worldwide. The literature on this topic indicates the importance of measuring technology transfer for all stakeholders, but on the other hand, providing practical performance assessments is still a significant challenge for all technology transfer stakeholders as well. Different institutions use different primarily quantitative indicators, such as number of innovations, number of patents, the total number of licenses, number of active licenses, number of spin-off companies, number of concluded research contracts, total license revenue, number of TTO's employees, the value of sponsored research expenditures, etc.

We argue that the university-industry/business relationship during technology transfer can take place in many different ways and affects many stakeholders. Therefore, the choice of indicators focused on a narrow range of activities and influences may limit the ability of universities and industry and business sectors to present their interests and performance in the technology transfer process. Considering the goal of such indicators: to assess technology transfer and TTO's effectiveness, this would affect TTO funding in turn. It opens up the possibility of exaggerating the numbers and their significance, without attempting to create mechanisms for assessing the quantity, but also the quality of indicators and measured results. For example, a university and its TTO may have few spin-offs, but they can create more positive economic and social benefits for the community that the university with more spin-offs.

In order to develop an effective TTO, universities should clearly define the TTO's role in the context of the economic and overall environment of the university. Universities must emphasize the role of TTO in achieving the economic and overall goals of the university. The governing bodies of the universities should intensify the cooperation between the different units of the universities and the TTO, clearly state

释放大学和企业潜力的工具，有助于经济增长、社会进步和文化发展。因此，当人们思考和讨论技术转移办公室时，需要考虑技术转移办公室对当地以及世界各地的影响。

关于哪些指标最适合衡量技术转移和技术转移在技术转移活动中的有效性的问题，全世界的研究仍然相对不足。这一专题的研究文献一方面表明了衡量技术转移对所有利益攸关方的重要性，但另一方面，提供实际业绩评估对所有技术转移利益攸关方来说仍然是一个重大挑战。不同的机构使用不同的主要定量指标，如创新数量、专利数量、许可证总数、有效许可证数量、分公司数量、签订的研究合同数量、许可证总收入、技术转移办公室的雇员人数和赞助研究支出的价值等。

我们认为，技术转移过程中的大学和产业/企业的关系可以采取不同种形式，并影响到许多利益相关者。因此，侧重于范围狭窄的活动和影响的选择指标，可能会限制大学、产业和商业部门在技术转移过程中展示其兴趣和业绩的能力。这些指标是为了评估技术转移和技术转移办公室的有效性，反过来也会影响技术转移办公室的资金。而这些指标没有试图建立评估数量的机制，也没有建立评估指标和衡量结果质量的机制，有夸大数字及其重要性的可能性。例如一所大学及其技术转移办公室可能没有什么附带利益，但它们可以为拥有更多附带利益大学的社会创造良好的经济效益和社会效益。

为了使技术转移办公室能够高效的发挥作用，大学应明确界定技术转移办公室在大学经济和整体环境中的作用。大学必须重视技术转移办公室在实现大学的经济和总体目标方面的作用。各大学的管理机构应加强大学各单位与技术转移办公室之间的合作，明确说明对这种合作的期望，并促

the expectations from that cooperation, and stimulate that cooperation. University governing bodies need to reinforce the concept that technology transfer is a resource for the benefit of the university and students, that TTOs are valued service providers and that TTOs are a potential channel for other sources of research funding. TTOs could play a leading role in connecting inventions with business. A fully functioning TTO means expenses in money and time. But TTO also contributes multiple benefits, which should take part when assessing TTO as a worthwhile investment.

TTOs are the needed and useful link between innovation and industry, which leads to different types of development in various areas, but always in favor of the people, state and regions. The research so far has shown that the TTOs are in function of the sustainable development of universities and the economy, and their establishment and development will involve the country in the world trends. States should cooperate in the international transfer of technologies and create international TTOs in order to create and promote economic growth and development throughout the world, especially in developing countries.

The insights from our research allow us to make suggestions for policy and practice. Namely, the state's political solutions and legislation must be coherent, transparent, clearly defined and applied consistently. On the other hand, universities' and other research organizations' management must try to make a balance between teaching and research. Strategic planning should be a roadmap for states and research organizations in achieving TTO effectiveness. We recommend the creation of networks of TTOs around the world with the potential to share ideas and booster research-industry interactions, with aims to improve life.

进这种合作。大学管理机构需要加强以下认识：技术转移是有利于大学和学生的资源，是重要的服务提供者；技术转移过程是其他研究资金来源的潜在渠道。技术转移办公室可以在将发明与商业联系起来方面发挥主导作用。充分运作的技术转移办公室意味着金钱和时间上的开支。但是，技术转移办公室也贡献了多种好处，技术转移办公室是一项有价值的投资。

技术转移办公室是创新和产业之间的必要且有用的纽带。它促进了不同领域、不同类型的产学研联合发展，有利于人民、地区和国家。到目前为止的研究表明，技术转移办公室是大学和企业可持续发展的助推剂，它们的建立和发展将使国家参与世界发展与进步。各国应在技术的国际转移方面进行合作，并建立国际贸易机会，以便在全世界，特别是发展中国家，创造和促进经济的增长和发展。

研究的深入了解使我们能够为政策和实践提出建议。也就是说，一方面，国家政治层面的解决办法和立法必须是一致的、透明的、界定明确的和适用的。另一方面，大学和其他研究组织必须努力在教学和研究之间取得平衡。战略规划应该为国家和研究组织实现技术转移办公室的有效性提供指导方针。因此，我们建议，在世界各地建立具有分享想法的，能够促进产学研互动潜力提升的技术转移办公室，以促进科技和经济的发展和繁荣。